The Blue-Grass Region of Kentucky

AND OTHER ARTICLES

OLD STONE HOMESTEAD

The Blue-Grass Region of Kentucky

AND OTHER KENTUCKY ARTICLES

BY
JAMES LANE ALLEN

ILLUSTRATED

Essay Index Reprint Series

BOOKS FOR LIBRARIES PRESS
FREEPORT, NEW YORK

LIBRARY
WAYNE STATE COLLEGE
WAYNE, NEBRASKA

First Published 1892
Reprinted 1972

Library of Congress Cataloging in Publication Data

Allen, James Lane, 1849-1925.
  The Blue-grass region of Kentucky.

  (Essay index reprint series)
  Reprint of the 1892 ed.
  CONTENTS: The Blue-grass region.--Uncle Tom at home.--County court day in Kentucky. [etc.]
  1. Kentucky--Social life and customs. I. Title.
F451.A65 1972   917.69'03'3   74-39712
ISBN 0-8369-2734-6

PRINTED IN THE UNITED STATES OF AMERICA
BY
NEW WORLD BOOK MANUFACTURING CO., INC.
HALLANDALE, FLORIDA 33009

PREFACE

The articles herein reprinted from *Harper's* and *The Century* magazines represent work done at intervals during the period that the author was writing the tales already published under the title of *Flute and Violin*.

It was his plan that with each descriptive article should go a short story dealing with the same subject, and this plan was in part wrought out. Thus, with the article entitled "Uncle Tom at Home" goes the tale entitled "Two Gentlemen of Kentucky"; and with the article entitled "A Home of the Silent Brotherhood" goes the tale entitled "The White Cowl." In the same way, there were to be short stories severally dealing with the other subjects embraced in this volume. But having in part wrought out this plan, the author has let it rest—not finally, perhaps, but because in the mean time he has found himself engaged with other themes.

J. L. A.

CONTENTS

	PAGE
THE BLUE-GRASS REGION	3
UNCLE TOM AT HOME	45
COUNTY COURT DAY IN KENTUCKY	87
KENTUCKY FAIRS	117
A HOME OF THE SILENT BROTHERHOOD	149
HOMESTEADS OF THE BLUE-GRASS	181
THROUGH CUMBERLAND GAP ON HORSEBACK	217
MOUNTAIN PASSES OF THE CUMBERLAND	249

ILLUSTRATIONS

OLD STONE HOMESTEAD	.	*Frontispiece*
SHEEP IN WOODLAWN PASTURE	.	*Facing p.* 6
NEGRO CABINS	.	" 14
CATTLE IN BLUE-GRASS PASTURE	.	" 18
HARRODSBURG PIKE	.	" 30
THE MAMMY	.	" 58
THE COOK	.	" 64
THE PREACHER	.	" 78
COURT-HOUSE SQUARE, LEXINGTON, KENTUCKY	.	" 94
THE "TICKLER"	.	" 96
GENTLEMEN OF LEISURE	.	" 108
HARNESS HORSES	.	" 132
A FORTNIGHTLY SHAVE	.	" 166
OLD FERRY AT POINT BURNSIDE	.	" 218
NATIVE TYPES	.	" 228
FORD ON THE CUMBERLAND	.	" 274

THE BLUE-GRASS REGION

I

ONE might well name it Saxon grass, so much is it at home in Saxon England, so like the loveliest landscapes of green Saxon England has it made other landscapes on which dwell a kindred race in America, and so akin is it to the type of nature that is peculiarly Saxon: being a hardy, kindly, beautiful, nourishing stock; loving rich lands and apt to find out where they lie; uprooting inferior aborigines, but stoutly defending its new domain against all invaders; paying taxes well, with profits to boot; thriving best in temperate latitudes and checkered sunshine; benevolent to flocks and herds; and allying itself closely to the history of any people whose content lies in simple plenty and habitual peace—the perfect squire-and-yeoman type of grasses.

In the earliest spring nothing is sooner afield to contest possession of the land than the bluegrass. Its little green spear-points are the first

The Blue-Grass Region

to pierce the soft rich earth, and array themselves in countless companies over the rolling landscapes, while its roots reach out in every direction for securer foothold. So early does this take place, that a late hoar-frost will now and then mow all these bristling spear-points down. Sometimes a slow-falling sleet will incase each emerald blade in glittering silver ; but the sun by-and-by melts the silver, leaving the blade unhurt. Or a light snowfall will cover tufts of it over, making pavilions and colonnades with white roofs resting on green pillars. The roofs vanish anon, and the columns go on silently rising. But usually the final rigors of the season prove harmless to the blue-grass. One sees it most beautiful in the spring, just before the seed stalks have shot upward from the flowing tufts, and while the thin, smooth, polished blades, having risen to their greatest height, are beginning to bend, or break and fall over on themselves and their nether fellows from sheer luxuriance. The least observant eye is now constrained to note that blue-grass is the characteristic element of the Kentucky turf — the first element of beauty in the Kentucky landscape. Over the stretches of woodland pasture, over the meadows and the lawns, by the edges of turnpike and lane, in the fence corners — wherever its seed has been allowed

The Blue-Grass Region

to flourish—its spreads a verdure so soft in fold and fine in texture, so entrancing by its freshness and fertility, that it looks like a deep-lying, thick-matted emerald moss. One thinks of it, not as some heavy, velvet-like carpet spread over the earth, but as some light, seamless veil that has fallen delicately around it, and that might be blown away by a passing breeze.

After this you will not see the blue-grass so beautiful. The seed ripens in June. Already the slender seed stalks have sprung up above the uniform green level, bearing on their summits the fuzzy, plumy, purplish seed-vessels; and save the soft, feathery undulations of these as the wind sweeps over them, the beauty of the blue-grass is gone. Moreover, certain robust and persistent weeds and grasses have been growing apace, roughening and diversifying the sward, so that the vista is less charming. During July and August the blue-grass lies comparatively inactive, resting from fructification, and missing, as well, frequent showers to temper the sunshine. In seasons of severe drought it even dies quite away, leaving the surface of the earth as bare and brown as a winter landscape or arid plain. Where it has been closely grazed, one may, in walking over it, stir such a dust as one would raise on

The Blue-Grass Region

a highway; and the upturned, half-exposed rootlets seem entirely dead. But the moderated heats and the gentle rains that usually come with the passing of summer bring on a second vigorous growth, and in the course of several weeks the landscape is covered with a verdure rivalling the luxuriance of spring.

There is something incongruous in this marvellous autumnal rejuvenescence of the bluegrass. All nature appears content and resting. The grapes on the sunward slopes have received their final coloring of purple and gold; the heavy mast is beginning to drop in the forest, followed by the silent lapse of russet and crimson leaves; the knee-deep aftermath has paled its green in the waiting autumn fields; the plump children are stretching out their nut-stained hands towards the first happy fire-glow on chill, dark evenings; and the cricket has left the sere, dead garden for a winter home at the hearth. Then, lo! as if by some freakish return of the spring to the edge of winter the pastures are suddenly as fresh and green as those of May. The effect on one who has the true landscape passion is transporting and bewildering. Such contrasts of color it is given one to study nowhere but in blue-grass lands. It is as if the seasons were met to do some great piece of brocading.

SHEEP IN WOODLAND PASTURE

The Blue-Grass Region

One sees a new meaning in Poe's melancholy thought — the leaves of the many-colored grass.

All winter the blue-grass continues green — it is always *green*, of course, never *blue* — and it even grows a little, except when the ground is frozen. Thus, year after year, drawing needful nourishment from the constantly disintegrating limestone below, flourishes here as nowhere else in the world this wonderful grass.

Even while shivering in the bleak winds of March, the young lambs frolicked away from the distent teats of the ewes, with growing relish for its hardy succulence, and by-and-by they were taken into market the sooner and the fatter for its developing qualities. During the long summer, foaming pails of milk and bowls of golden butter have testified to the Kentucky housewife with what delight the cows have ruminated on the stores gathered each plentiful day. The Kentucky farmer knows that the distant metropolitan beef-eater will in time have good reason to thank it for yonder winding herd of sleek young steers that are softly brushing their rounded sides with their long, white, silky tails, while they plunge their puffing noses into its depths and tear away huge mouthfuls of its inexhaustible richness. Thorough-bred sire and dam and

The Blue-Grass Region

foal in paddocks or deeper pastures have drawn from it form and quality and organization: hardness and solidity of bone, strength of tendon, firmness and elasticity of muscle, power of nerve, and capacity of lung. Even the Falstaff porkers, their eyes gleaming with gluttonous enjoyment, have looked to it for the shaping of their posthumous hams and the padding of their long backbones in depths of snowy lard. In winter mules and sheep and horses paw away the snow to get at the green shoots that lie covered over beneath the full, rank growth of autumn, or they find it attractive provender in their ricks. For all that live upon it, it is perennial and abundant, beautiful and beneficent—the first great natural factor in the prosperity of the Kentucky people. What wonder if the Kentuckian, like the Greek of old, should wish to have even his paradise well set in grass; or that, with a knowing humor, he should smile at David for saying, "He maketh his grass to grow upon the mountains," inasmuch as the only grass worth speaking of grows on his beloved plain!

II

BUT if grass is the first element in the lovely Kentucky landscape, as it must be in every other one, by no means should it be thought sole or chief. In Dante, as Ruskin points out, whenever the country is to be beautiful, we come into open air and open meadows. Homer places the sirens in a meadow when they are to sing. Over the blue-grass, therefore, one walks into the open air and open meadows of the blue-grass land.

This has long had reputation for being one of the very beautiful spots of the earth, and it is worth while to consider those elements of natural scenery wherein the beauty consists.

One might say, first, that the landscape possesses what is so very rare even in beautiful landscapes—the quality of gracefulness. Nowhere does one encounter vertical lines or violent slopes; nor are there perfectly level stretches like those that make the green fields monotonous in the Dutch lowlands. The dark,

The Blue-Grass Region

finely sifted soil lies deep over the limestone hills, filling out their chasms to evenness, and rounding their jagged or precipitous edges, very much as a heavy snow at night will leave the morning landscape with mitigated ruggedness and softer curves. The long, slow action of water has further moulded everything into symmetry, so that the low ancient hills descend to the valleys in exquisite folds and uninterrupted slopes. The whole great plain undulates away league after league towards the distant horizon in an endless succession of gentle convex surfaces—like the easy swing of the sea—presenting a panorama of subdued swells and retiring surges. Everything in the blue-grass country is billowy and afloat. The spirit of nature is intermediate between violent energy and complete repose; and the effect of this mild activity is kept from monotony by the accidental perspective of position, creating variety of details.

One traces this quality of gracefulness in the labyrinthine courses of the restful streams, in the disposition of forest masses, in the free, unstudied succession of meadow, field, and lawn. Surely it is just this order of low hill scenery, just these buoyant undulations, that should be covered with the blue-grass. Had Hawthorne ever looked on this landscape when most beau-

The Blue-Grass Region

tiful, he could never have said of England that "no other country will ever have this charm of lovely verdure." Characteristically beautiful spots on the blue-grass landscape are the woodland pastures. A Kentucky wheat-field, a Kentucky meadow, a Kentucky lawn, is but a field, a meadow, a lawn, found elsewhere; but a Kentucky sylvan slope has a loveliness unique and local. Rightly do poets make pre-eminently beautiful countries abound in trees. John Burroughs, writing with enthusiasm of English woods, has said that "in midsummer the hair of our trees seems to stand on end; the woods have a frightened look, or as if they were just recovering from a debauch." This is not true of the Kentucky woods, unless it be in some season of protracted drought. The foliage of the Kentucky trees is not thin nor dishevelled, the leaves crowd thick to the very ends of the boughs, and spread themselves full to the sky, making, where they are close together, under-spaces of green gloom scarcely shot through by sunbeams. Indeed, one often finds here the perfection of tree forms. I mean that rare development which brings the extremities of the boughs to the very limit of the curve that nature intends the tree to define as the peculiar shape of its species. Any

The Blue-Grass Region

but the most favorable conditions leave the outline jagged, faulty, and untrue. Here and there over the blue-grass landscape one's eye rests on a cone-shaped, or dome-shaped, or inverted pear-shaped, or fan-shaped tree. Nor are fulness of leafage and perfection of form alone to be noted; pendency of boughs is another distinguishing feature. One who loves and closely studies trees will note here the comparative absence of woody stiffness. It is expected that the willow and the elm should droop their branches. Here the same characteristic strikes you in the wild cherry, the maple, and the sycamore—even in great walnuts and ashes and oaks; and I have occasionally discovered exceeding grace of form in hackberries (which usually look paralytic and as if waiting to hobble away on crutches), in locusts, and in the harsh hickories—loved by Thoreau.

But to return to the woodland pastures. They are the last vestiges of that unbroken primeval forest which, together with canebrakes and pea-vines, covered the face of the country when it was first beheld by the pioneers. No blue-grass then. In these woods the timber has been so cut out that the remaining trees often stand clearly revealed in their entire form, their far-reaching boughs perhaps not even

The Blue-Grass Region

touching those of their nearest neighbor, or interlacing them with ineffectual fondness. There is something pathetic in the sight, and in the thought of those innumerable stricken ones that in years agone were dismembered for cord-wood and kitchen stoves and the vast fireplaces of old-time negro cabins. In the well-kept blue-glass pasture undergrowth and weeds are annually cut down, so that the massive trunks are revealed from a distance ; the better because the branches seldom are lower than ten to twenty feet above the earth. Thus in its daily course the sun strikes every point beneath the broad branches, and nourishes the blue-grass up to the very roots. All savagery, all wildness, is taken out of these pastures ; they are full of tenderness and repose—of the utmost delicacy and elegance. Over the graceful earth spreads the flowing green grass, uniform and universal. Above this stand the full, swelling trunks—warm browns and pale grays —often lichen-flecked or moss-enamelled. Over these expand the vast domes and canopies of leafage. And falling down upon these comes the placid sunshine through a sky of cerulean blueness, and past the snowy zones of gleaming cloud. The very individuality of the tree comes out as it never can in denser places. Always the most truly human object in still, voiceless

The Blue-Grass Region

nature, it here throws out its arms to you with imploring tenderness, with what Wadsworth called "the soft eye-music of slow-waving boughs." One cannot travel far in the blue-grass country without coming upon one of these woodland strips.

Of the artistic service rendered the landscape of this region by other elements of scenery—atmosphere and cloud and sky—much might, but little will, be said. The atmosphere is sometimes crystalline, sometimes full of that intense repose of dazzling light which one, without ever having seen them, knows to be on canvases of Turner. Then, again, it is amber-hued, or tinged with soft blue, graduated to purple shadows on the horizon. During the greater part of the year the cloud-sky is one of strongly outlined forms; the great white cumuli drift over, with every majesty of design and grace of grouping; but there come, in milder seasons, many days when one may see three cloud belts in the heavens at the same time, the lowest far, far away, and the highest brushing softly, as it were, past the very dome of the inviolable blue. You turn your eye downward to see the light wandering wistfully among the low distant hills, and the sweet tremulous shadows crossing the meadows with timid cadences. It *is* a beautiful country; the Kentucky skies are not

NEGRO CABINS

The Blue-Grass Region

the cold, hard, brilliant, hideous things that so many writers on nature style American skies (usually meaning New England skies), as contrasted with skies European. They are at times ineffably warm in tone and tender in hue, giving aerial distances magical and fathomless above, and throwing down upon the varied soft harmonious greens of the landscape below, upon its rich browns and weathered grays and whole scheme of terrene colors, a flood of radiance as bountiful and transfiguring as it is chastened and benign.

But why make a description of the blue-grass region of Kentucky? What one sees may be only what one feels—only intricate affinities between nature and self that were developed long ago, and have become too deep to be viewed as relations or illusions. What two human beings find the same things in the face of a third, or in nature's? Descriptions of scenery are notoriously disappointing to those whose taste in landscape is different, or who have little or no sentiment for pure landscape beauty. So one coming hither might be sorely disappointed. No mountains; no strips of distant blue gleaming water nor lawny cascades; no grandeur; no majesty; no wild picturesqueness. The chords of landscape harmony are very simple; nothing but softness and amenity,

The Blue-Grass Region

grace and repose, delicacy and elegance. One might fail at seasons to find even these. This is a beautiful country, but not always; there come days when the climate shows as ugly a temper as possible. Not a little of the finest timber has been lost by storms. The sky is for days one great blanket of grewsome gray. In winter you laugh with chattering teeth at those who call this "the South," the thermometer perhaps registering from twelve to fifteen degrees below zero. In summer the name is but a half-truth. Only by visiting this region during some lovely season, or by dwelling here from year to year, and seeing it in all the humors of storm and sunshine, can one love it.

III

BUT the ideal landscape of daily life must not be merely beautiful: it should be useful. With what may not the fertility of this region be compared? With the valleys of the Schuylkill, the Shenandoah, and the Genesee; with the richest lands of Lombardy and Belgium; with the most fertile districts of England. The evidences of this fertility are everywhere. Nature, even in those places where she has been forced for nearly a hundred years to bear much at the hands of a not always judicious agriculture, unceasingly struggles to cover herself with bushes of all sorts and nameless annual weeds and grasses. Even the blue-grass contends in vain for complete possession of its freehold. One is forced to note, even though without sentiment, the rich pageant of transitory wild bloom that *will* force a passage for itself over the landscape : firmaments of golden dandelions in the lawns; vast beds of violets, gray and blue, in dim

The Blue-Grass Region

glades; patches of flaunting sunflowers along the road-sides; purple thistles; and, of deeper purple still and far denser growth, beautiful ironweed in the woods; with many clumps of alder bloom, and fast-extending patches of perennial blackberry, and groups of delicate May-apples, and whole fields of dog-fennel and goldenrod. And why mention indomitable dock and gigantic poke, burrs and plenteous nightshade, and mullein and plantain, with dusty gray-green ragweed and thrifty foxtail?—an innumerable company.

Maize, pumpkins, and beans grow together in a field—a triple crop. Nature perfects them all, yet must do more. Scarce have the ploughs left the furrows before there springs up a varied wild growth, and a fourth crop, morning-glories, festoon the tall tassels of the Indian-corn ere the knife can be laid against the stalk. Harvest fields usually have their stubble well hidden by a rich, deep aftermath. Garden patches, for all that hoe and rake can do, commonly look at last like spots given over to weeds and grasses. Sidewalks quickly lose their borders. Pavements would soon disappear from sight; the winding of a distant stream through the fields can be readily followed by the line of vegetation that rushes there to fight for life, from the minutest creeping vines to forest

CATTLE IN BLUE-GRASS PASTURE.

The Blue-Grass Region

trees. Every neglected fence corner becomes an area for a fresh colony. Leave one of these sweet, humanized woodland pastures alone for a shore period of years, it runs wild with a dense young natural forest ; vines shoot up to the tops of the tallest trees, and then tumble over in green sprays on the heads of others.

A kind, true, patient, self-helpful soil if ever there was one! Some of these lands after being cultivated, not always scientifically, but always without artificial fertilizers, for more than three-quarters of a century, are now, if properly treated, equal in productiveness to the best farming lands of England. The farmer from one of these old fields will take two different crops in a season. He gets two cuttings of clover from a meadow, and has rich grazing left. A few counties have at a time produced three-fourths of the entire hemp product of the United States. The State itself has at different times stood first in wheat and hemp and Indian-corn and wool and tobacco and flax, although half its territory is covered with virgin forests. When lands under improper treatment have become impoverished, their productiveness has been restored, not by artificial fertilizers, but by simple rotation of crops, with nature's help. The soil rests on decomposable limestone, which annually gives

The Blue-Grass Region

up to it in solution all the essential mineral plant food that judicious agriculture needs.

Soil and air and climate—the entire aggregate of influences happily co-operative—make the finest grazing. The Kentucky horse has carried the reputation of the country into regions where even the people could never have made it known. Your expert in the breeding of thoroughbreds will tell you that the muscular fibre of the blue-grass animal is to that of the Pennsylvania-bred horses as silk to cotton, and the texture of his bone, compared with the latter's, as ivory beside pumice-stone. If taken to the Eastern States, in twelve generations he is no longer the same breed of horse. His blood fertilizes American stock the continent over. Jersey cattle brought here increase in size. Sires come to Kentucky to make themselves and their offspring famous.

The people themselves are a fecund race. Out of this State have gone more to enrich the citizenship of the nation than all the other States together have been able to send into it. So at least your loyal-hearted Kentuckian looks at the rather delicate subject of inter-State migration. By actual measurement the Kentucky volunteers during the Civil War were found to surpass all others (except Tennessee-

The Blue-Grass Region

ans) in height and weight, whether coming from the United States or various countries of Europe. But for the great-headed Scandinavians, they would have been first, also, in circumference around the forehead and occiput. Still, Kentucky has little or no literature.

One element that should be conspicuous in fertile countries does not strike the observer here—much beautiful water; no other State has a frontage of navigable rivers equal to that of Kentucky. But there are few limpid, lovely, smaller streams. Wonderful springs there are, and vast stores of water in the cavernous earth below; but the landscape lacks the charm of this element—clear, rushing, musical, abundant. The watercourses, ever winding and graceful, are apt to be either swollen and turbid or insignificant; of late years the beds seem less full also—a change consequent, perhaps, upon the denudation of forest lands. In a dry season the historic Elkhorn seems little more than a ganglion of precarious pools.

IV

THE best artists who have painted cultivated ground have always been very careful to limit the area of the crops. Undoubtedly the substitution of a more scientific agriculture for the loose and easy ways of primitive husbandry has changed the key-note of rural existence from a tender Virgilian sentiment to a coarser strain, and as life becomes more unsophisticated it grows less picturesque. When the work of the old-time reaper is done by a fat man with a flaming face, sitting on a cast-iron machine, and smoking a cob pipe, the artist will leave the fields. Figures have a terrible power to destroy sentiment in pure landscape; so have houses. When one leaves nature, pure and simple, in the blue-grass country, he must accordingly pick his way circumspectly or go amiss in his search for the beautiful. If his taste lead him to desire in landscapes the finest evidences of human labor, the high artificial finish of a minutely careful civilization,

The Blue-Grass Region

he will here find great disappointment. On the other hand, if he delight in those exquisite rural spots of the Old World with picturesque bits of homestead architecture and the perfection of horticultural and unobtrusive botanical details, he will be no less aggrieved. What he sees here is neither the most scientific farming, simply economic and utilitarian—raw and rude—nor that cultivated desire for the elements in nature to be so moulded by the hand of man that they will fuse harmoniously and inextricably with his habitations and his work.

The whole face of the country is taken up by a succession of farms. Each of these, except the very small ones, presents to the eye the variation of meadow, field, and woodland pasture, together with the homestead and the surrounding grounds of orchard, garden, and lawn. The entire landscape is thus caught in a vast net-work of fences. The Kentuckian retains his English ancestors' love of enclosures; but the uncertain tenure of estates beyond a single generation does not encourage him to make them the most durable. One does, indeed, notice here and there throughout the country stone-walls of blue limestone, that give an aspect of substantial repose and comfortable firmness to the scenery. But the farmer dreads their costliness, even though his own hill-sides

The Blue-Grass Region

furnish him an abundant quarry. He knows that unless the foundations are laid like those of a house, the thawing earth will unsettle them, that water, freezing as it trickles through the crevices, will force the stones out of their places, and that breaches will be made in them by boys on a hunt whenever and wherever it shall be necessary to get at a lurking or sorely pressed hare. It is ludicrously true that the most terrible destroyer of stone-walls in this country is the small boy hunting a hare, with an appetite for game that knows no geological impediment. Therefore one hears of fewer limestone fences of late years, some being torn down and superseded by plank fences or post-and-rail fences, or by the newer barbed-wire fence—an economic device that will probably become as popular in regions where stone and timber were never to be had as in others, like this, where timber has been ignorantly, wantonly sacrificed. It is a pleasure to know that one of the most expensive, and certainly the most hideous, fences ever in vogue here is falling into disuse. I mean the worm-fence—called worm because it wriggled over the landscape like a long brown caterpillar, the stakes being the bristles along its back, and because it now and then ate up a noble walnut-tree close by, or a kingly oak, or frightened, trembling ash—a worm that decided

The Blue-Grass Region

the destiny of forests. A pleasure it is, too, to come occasionally upon an Osage orange hedgerow, which is a green eternal fence. But you will not find many of these. It is generally too much to ask of an American, even though he be a Kentuckian, to wait for a hedge to grow and make him a fence. When he takes a notion to have a fence, he wants it put up before Saturday night.

If the Kentuckian, like the Englishman, is fond of fencing himself off, like the Frenchman, he loves long, straight roads. You will not find elsewhere in America such highways as the Kentuckian has constructed over his country — broad, smooth, level, white, glistening turnpikes of macadamized limestone. It is a luxury to drive, and also an expense, as one will discover before one has passed through many toll-gates. One could travel more cheaply on the finest railway on the continent. What Richard Grant White thought it worth while to record as a rare and interesting sight—a man on an English highway breaking stones—is no uncommon sight here. All limestone for these hundreds of miles of road, having been quarried here, there, anywhere, and carted and strewn along the road-side, is broken by a hammer in the hand. By the highway the workman sits—usually an Irish-

The Blue-Grass Region

man—pecking away at a long rugged pile as though he were good to live for a thousand years. Somehow, in patience, he always gets to the other end of his hard row.

One cannot sojourn long without coming to conceive an interest in this limestone, and loving to meet its rich warm hues on the landscape. It has made a deal of history: limestone blue-grass, limestone water, limestone roads, limestone fences, limestone bridges and arches, limestone engineering architecture, limestone water-mills, limestone spring-houses and homesteads — limestone Kentuckians! Outside of Scripture no people was ever so founded on a rock. It might be well to note, likewise, that the soil of this region is what scientists call sedentary—called so because it sits quietly on the rocks, not because the people sit quietly on it.

Undoubtedly the most picturesque monuments in the blue-grass country are old stone water-mills and old stone homesteads — landmarks each for separate trains of ideas that run to poetry and to history. The latter, built by pioneers or descendants of pioneers, nearly a hundred years ago, stand gray with years, but good for nameless years to come; great low chimneys, deep little windows, thick walls, mighty fireplaces; situated usually with keen

The Blue-Grass Region

discretion on an elevation near a spring, just as a Saxon forefather would have placed them centuries ago. Haply one will see the water of this spring issuing still from a recess in a hill-side, with an overhanging ledge of rock— the entrance to this cavern being walled across and closed with a gate, thus making, according to ancient fashion, a simple natural spring-house and dairy.

Something like a feeling of exasperation is apt to come over one in turning to the typical modern houses. Nowhere, certainly, in rural America, are there, within the same area, more substantial, comfortable homesteads. They are nothing if not spacious and healthful, frame or brick, two stories, shingle roofs. But they lack characteristic physiognomy; they have no harmony with the landscape, nor with each other, nor often with themselves. They are not beautiful when new, and can never be beautiful when old; for the beauty of newness and the beauty of oldness alike depend on beauty of form and color, which here is lacking. One longs for the sight of a rural Gothic cottage, which would harmonize so well with the order of the scenery, or for a light, elegant villa that should overlook these light and elegant undulations of a beautiful and varied landscape. It must be

The Blue-Grass Region

understood that there are notable exceptions to these statements even in the outlying districts of the blue-grass country, and that they do not apply to the environs of the towns, nor to the towns themselves.

Nowhere does one see masses of merely beautiful things in the country. The slumbering art of interior decoration is usually spent upon the parlor. The grounds around the houses are not kept in the best order. The typical rural Kentucky housewife does not seem to have any compelling, controlling sense of the beautiful. She invariably concedes something to beauty, but not enough. You will find a show of flowers at the poorest houses, though but geranium slips in miscellaneous tins and pottery. But you do not generally see around more prosperous homes any such parterres or beds as there is money to spend on, and time to tend, and grounds to justify.

A like spirit is shown by the ordinary blue-grass farmer. His management strikes you as not the pink of tidiness, not the model of systematic thrift. Exceptions exist—many exceptions—but the rule holds good. One cannot travel here in summer or autumn without observing that weeds flourish where they harm and create ugliness; fences go unrepaired;

The Blue-Grass Region

gates may be found swinging on one hinge. He misuses his long-cultivated fields; he cuts down his scant, precious trees. His energy is not tireless, his watchfulness not sleepless. Why should they be? Human life here is not massed and swarming. The occupation of the soil is not close and niggard. The landscape is not even compact, much less crowded. There is room for more, plenty for more to eat. No man here, like the ancient Roman prætor, ever decided how often one might, without trespass, gather the acorns that fall from his neighbors' trees. No woman ever went through a blue-grass harvest-field gleaning. Ruth's vocation is unknown. By nature the Kentuckian is no rigid economist. By birth, education, tradition, and inherited tendencies he is not a country clout, but a rural gentleman. His ideal of life is neither vast wealth nor personal distinction, but solid comfort in material conditions, and the material conditions are easy: fertility of soil, annual excess of production over consumption, comparative thinness of population. So he does not brace himself for the tense struggle of life as it goes on in centres of fierce territorial shoulder-pushing. He can afford to indulge his slackness of endeavor. He is neither an alert aggressive agriculturist, nor a landscape-

The Blue-Grass Region

gardener, nor a purveyor of commodities to the green-grocer. If the world wants vegetables, let it raise them. He declines to work himself to death for other people, though they pay him for it. He wife is a lady, not a domestic laborer; and it is her privilege, in household affairs, placidly to surround herself with an abundance which the life-long female economists of the North would regard with conscientious indignation.

In truth, there is much evidence to show that this park-like country, intersected by many beautiful railroads, turnpikes, and shaded picturesque lanes, will become less and less an agricultural district, more and more a region of unequalled pasturage, and hence more park-like still. One great interest abides here, of course—the manufacture of Bourbon whiskey. Another interest has only within the last few years been developed—the cultivation of tobacco, for which it was formerly thought that the blue-grass soils were not adapted. But as years go by, the stock interests invite more capital, demand more attention, give more pleasure—in a word, strike the full chord of modern interest by furnishing an unparalleled means of speculative profit.

Forty years ago the most distinguished citizens of the State were engaged in writing es-

HARRODSBURG PIKE

The Blue-Grass Region

says and prize papers on scientific agriculture. A regular trotting track was not to be found in the whole country. Nothing was thought of the breeding and training of horses with reference to development of greater speed. Pacing horses were fashionable; and two great rivals in this gait having been brought together for a trial of speed, in lieu of a track, paced a mighty race over a river-bottom flat. We have changed all that. The gentlemen no longer write their essays. Beef won the spurs of knighthood. In Kentucky the horse has already been styled the first citizen. The great agricultural fairs of the State have modified their exhibits with reference to him alone, and fifteen or twenty thousand people give afternoon after afternoon to the contemplation of his beauty and his speed. His one rival is the thoroughbred, who goes on running faster and faster. One of the brief code of nine laws for the government of the young Kentucky commonwealth that were passed in the first legislative assembly ever held west of the Alleghanies dealt with the preservation of the breed of horses. Nothing was said of education. The Kentuckian loves the memory of Thomas Jefferson, not forgetting that he once ran race-horses. These great interests, not overlooking the cattle interest, the manufacture of whiskey, and the raising of to-

The Blue-Grass Region

bacco, will no doubt constitute the future determining factors in the history of this country. It should not be forgotten, however, that the Northern and Eastern palate becomes kindly disposed at the bare mention of the many thousands of turkeys that annually fatten on these plains.

V

"IN Kentucky," writes Professor Shaler, in his recent history, "we shall find nearly pure English blood. It is, moreover, the largest body of pure English folk that has, speaking generally, been separated from the mother-country for two hundred years." They, the blue-grass Kentuckians, are the descendants of those hardy, high-spirited, picked Englishmen, largely of the squire and yeoman class, whose absorbing passion was not religious disputation, nor the intellectual purpose of founding a State, but the ownership of land and the pursuits and pleasures of rural life, close to the rich soil, and full of its strength and sunlight. They have to this day, in a degree perhaps equalled by no others living, the race qualities of their English ancestry and the tastes and habitudes of their forefathers. If one knows the Saxon nature, and has been a close student of Kentucky life and character, stripped bare of the accidental circumstances of local environ-

The Blue-Grass Region

ment, he may amuse himself with laying the two side by side and comparing the points of essential likeness. It is a question whether the Kentuckian is not more like his English ancestor than his New England contemporary. This is an old country, as things go in the West. The rock formation is very old; the soil is old; the race qualities here are old. In the Sagas, in the Edda, a man must be overbrave. "Let all who are not cowards follow me!" cried McGary, putting an end to prudent counsel on the eve of the battle of the Blue Licks. The Kentuckian winced under the implication then, and has done it in a thousand instances since. Over-bravery! The idea runs through the pages of Kentucky history, drawing them, back into the centuries of his race. It is this quality of temper and conception of manhood that has operated to build up in the mind of the world the figure of the typical Kentuckian. Hawthorne conversed with an old man in England who told him that the Kentuckians flayed Tecumseh where he fell, and converted his skin into razor-strops. Collins, the Kentucky Froissart, speaking of Kentucky pioneers, relates of the father of one of them that he knocked Washington down in a quarrel, and received an apology from the Father of his Country on the following day. I have mentioned this typical

The Blue-Grass Region

Hotspur figure because I knew it would come foremost into the mind of the reader whenever one began to speak with candor of Kentucky life and character. It was never a true type: satire bit always into burlesque along lines of coarseness and exaggeration. Much less is it true now, except in so far as it describes a kind of human being found the world over. But I was saying that old race qualities are apparent here, because this is a people of English blood with hereditary agricultural tastes, and because it has remained to this day largely uncommingled with foreign strains. Here, for instance, is the old race conservatism that expends itself reverentially on established ways and familiar customs. The building of the first great turnpike in this country was opposed on the ground that it would shut up way-side taverns, throw wagons and teams out of employment, and destroy the market for chickens and oats. Prior to that, immigration was discouraged because it would make the already high prices of necessary articles so exorbitant that the permanent prosperity of the State would receive a fatal check. True, however, this opposition was not without a certain philosophy; for in those days people went to some distant lick for their salt, bought it warm from the kettle at seven or eight cents a pound, and

The Blue-Grass Region

packed it home on horseback, so that a fourth dropped away in bitter water. Coming back to the present, the huge yellowish-red stage-coach rolls to-day over the marbled roads of the blue-grass country. Families may be found living exactly where their pioneer ancestors effected a heroic settlement—a landed aristocracy, if there be such in America. Family names come down from generation to generation, just as a glance at the British peerage will show that they were long ago being transmitted in kindred families over the sea. One great honored name will do nearly as much in Kentucky as in England to keep a family in peculiar respect, after the reason for it has ceased. Here is that old invincible race ideal of personal liberty, and that old, unreckoning, truculent, animal rage at whatever infringes on it. The Kentuckians were among the very earliest to grant manhood suffrage. Nowhere in this country are the rights of property more inviolable, the violations of these more surely punished: neither counsel nor judge nor any power whatsoever can acquit a man who has taken fourpence of his neighbor's goods. Here is the old land-loving, land-holding, home-staying, home-defending disposition. This is not the lunching, tourist race that, to Mr. Ruskin's horror, leaves its crumbs and chicken-bones on

The Blue-Grass Region

the glaciers. The simple rural key-note of life is still the sweetest. Now, after the lapse of more than a century, the most populous town contains less than twenty thousand white souls. Along with the love of land has gone comparative content with the annual increase of flock and field. No man among them has ever got immense wealth. Here is the old sense of personal privacy and reserve which has for centuries intrenched the Englishman in the heart of his estate, and forced him to regard with inexpugnable discomfort his neighbor's boundaries. This would have been a densely peopled region, the farms would have been minutely subdivided, had sons asked and received permission to settle on parts of the ancestral estate. This filling in and too close personal contact would have satisfied neither father nor child, so that the one has generally kept his acres intact, and the other, impelled by the same land-hunger that brought his pioneer forefather hither, has gone hence into the younger West, where lie broader tracts and vaster spaces. Here is the old idea, somewhat current still in England, that the highest mark of the gentleman is not cultivation of the mind, not intellect, not knowledge, but elegant living. Here is the old hereditary devotion to the idea of the State. Write the biographies of the Kentuckians who

The Blue-Grass Region

have been engaged in national or in local politics, and you have largely the history of the State of Kentucky. Write the lives of all its scientists, artists, musicians, actors, poets, novelists, and you find many weary mile-stones between the chapters.

Enter the blue-grass region from what point you choose — and you may do this, so well traversed is it by railways—and you become sensitive to its influence. If you come from the North or the East, you say : "This is not modern America. Here is something local and unique. For one thing, nothing goes fast here." By-and-by you see a blue-grass race-horse, and note an exception. But you do not also except the rider or the driver. The speed is not his. He is a mere bunch of mistletoe to the horse. Detach him, and he is not worth timing. Human speed for the most part lies fallow. Every man starts for the goal of life at his own natural gait, and if he sees that it is too far off for him to reach it in a lifetime, he does not run the faster, but has the goal moved nearer him. The Kentuckians are not provincial. As Thoreau said, no people can long remain provincial who have a propensity for politics, whittling, and rapid travelling. They are not inaccessible to modern ideas, but the shock of modern ideas has not elec-

The Blue-Grass Region

trified them. They have walled themselves around with old race instincts and habitudes, and when the stream of tendency rushes against this wall, it recoils upon itself instead of sweeping away the barrier. The typical Kentuckian regards himself an American of the Americans, and thinks as little of being like the English as he would of imitating the Jutes. In nothing is he more like his transatlantic ancestry than in strong self-content. He sits on his farm as though it were the pole of the heavens — a manly man with a heart in him. Usually of the blond type, robust, well formed, with clear, fair complexion, that grows ruddier with age and stomachic development, full neck, and an open, kind, untroubled countenance. He is frank, but not familiar; talkative, but not garrulous; full of the genial humor of local hits and allusions, but without a subtle nimbleness of wit; indulgent towards purely masculine vices, but intolerant of petty crimes; no reader of books nor master in religious debate, faith coming to him as naturally as his appetite, and growing with what it feeds upon; loving roast pig, but not caring particularly for Lamb's eulogy; loving his grass like a Greek, not because it is beautiful, but because it is fresh and green; a peaceful man with

The Blue-Grass Region

strong passions, and so to be heartily loved and respected or heartily hated and respected, but never despised or trifled with. An occasional barbecue in the woods, where the saddles of South Down mutton are roasted on spits over the coals of the mighty trench, and the steaming kettles of burgoo lend their savor to the nose of the hungry political orator, so that he becomes all the more impetuous in his invectives; the great agricultural fairs; the race-courses; the monthly county court day, when he meets his neighbors on the public square of the nearest town; the quiet Sunday mornings, when he meets them again for rather more clandestine talks at the front door of the neighborhood church—these and his own fireside are his characteristic and ample pleasures. You will never be under his roof without being touched by the mellowest of all the virtues of his race—simple, unsparing human kindness and hospitality.

The women of Kentucky have long had reputation for beauty. An average type is a refinement on the English blonde—greater delicacy of form, feature, and color. A beautiful Kentucky woman is apt to be exceedingly beautiful. Her voice is low and soft; her hands and feet delicately formed; her skin pure and beautiful in tint and shading; her

The Blue-Grass Region

eyes blue or brown, and hair nut brown or golden brown; to all which is added a certain unapproachable refinement. It must not for a moment be supposed, however, that there are not many genuinely ugly women in Kentucky.

UNCLE TOM AT HOME

I

ON the outskirts of the towns of central Kentucky, a stranger, searching for the picturesque in architecture and in life, would find his attention arrested by certain masses of low frame and brick structures, and by the multitudes of strange human beings that inhabit them. A single town may have on its edges several of these settlements, which are themselves called "towns," and bear separate names either descriptive of some topographical peculiarity or taken from the original owners of the lots. It is in these that a great part of the negro population of Kentucky has packed itself since the war. Here live the slaves of the past with their descendants; old family servants from the once populous country places; old wagon-drivers from the deep-rutted lanes; old wood-choppers from the slaughtered bluegrass forests; old harvesters and ploughmen from the long since abandoned fields; old cooks from the savory, wasteful kitchens; old nurses

Uncle Tom at Home

from the softly rocked and softly sung-to cradles. Here, too, are the homes of the younger generation, of the laundresses and the barbers, teachers and ministers of the gospel, coachmen and porters, restaurant-keepers and vagabonds, hands from the hemp factories, and workmen on the outlying farms.

You step easily from the verge of the white population to the confines of the black. But it is a great distance—like the crossing of a vast continent between the habitats of alien races. The air seems all at once to tan the cheek. Out of the cold, blue recesses of the midsummer sky the sun burns with a fierceness of heat that warps the shingles of the pointed roofs and flares with blinding brilliancy against some whitewashed wall. Perhaps in all the street no little cooling stretch of shade. The unpaved sidewalks and the roadway between are but undistinguishable parts of a common thoroughfare, along which every upspringing green thing is quickly trodden to death beneath the ubiquitous play and passing of many feet. Here and there, from some shielded nook or other coign of vantage, a single plumy branch of dog-fennel may be seen spreading its small firmament of white and golden stars close to the ground; or between its pale green stalks the faint lavender of the nightshade will take

Uncle Tom at Home

the eye as the sole emblem of the flowering world.

A negro town! Looking out the doors and windows of the cabins, lounging in the doorways, leaning over the low frame fences, gathering into quickly forming, quickly dissolving groups in the dusty streets, they swarm. They are here from milk-white through all deepening shades to glossy blackness; octoroons, quadroons, mulattoes—some with large liquid black eyes, refined features, delicate forms; working, gossiping, higgling over prices around a vegetable cart, discussing last night's church festival, to-day's funeral, or next week's railway excursion, sleeping, planning how to get work and how to escape it. From some unseen old figure in flamboyant turban, bending over the wash-tub in the rear of a cabin, comes a crooned song of indescribable pathos; behind a half-closed front shutter, a Moorish-hued *amoroso* in gay linen thrums his banjo in a measure of ecstatic gayety preluding the more passionate melodies of the coming night. Here a fight; there the sound of the fiddle and the rhythmic patting of hands. Tatters and silks flaunt themselves side by side. Dirt and cleanliness lie down together. Indolence goes hand in hand with thrift. Superstition dogs the slow footsteps of reason. Passion and self-control eye

Uncle Tom at Home

each other across the narrow way. If there is anywhere resolute virtue, round it is a weltered muck of low and sensual desire. One sees the surviving types of old negro life here crowded together with and contrasted with the new phases of "colored" life—sees the transitional stage of a race, part of whom were born slaves and are now freemen, part of whom have been born freemen but remain so much like slaves.

It cannot fail to happen, as you walk along, that you will come upon some cabin set back in a small yard and half hidden, front and side, by an almost tropical jungle of vines and multiform foliage; patches of great sunflowers, never more leonine in tawny magnificence and sun-loving repose; festoons of white and purple morning-glories over the windows and up to the low eaves; around the porch and above the door-way, a trellis of gourd-vines swinging their long-necked, grotesque yellow fruit; about the entrance flaming hollyhocks and other brilliant bits of bloom, marigolds and petunias—evidences of the warm, native taste that still distinguishes the negro after some centuries of contact with the cold, chastened ideals of the Anglo-Saxon.

In the door-way of such a cabin, sheltered from the afternoon sun by his dense jungle of vines, but with a few rays of light glinting

Uncle Tom at Home

through the fluttering leaves across his seamed black face and white woolly head, the muscles of his once powerful arms shrunken, the gnarled hands folded idly in his lap—his occupation gone—you will haply see some old-time slave of the class of Mrs. Stowe's Uncle Tom. For it is true that scattered here and there throughout the negro towns of Kentucky are representatives of the same class that furnished her with her hero; true, also, that they were never sold by their Kentucky masters to the plantations of the South, but remained unsold down to the last days of slavery.

When the war scattered the negroes of Kentucky blindly, tumultuously, hither and thither, many of them gathered the members of their families about them and moved from the country into these "towns"; and here the few survivors live, ready to testify of their relations with their former masters and mistresses, and indirectly serving to point a great moral: that, however justly Mrs. Stowe may have chosen one of their number as best fitted to show the fairest aspects of domestic slavery in the United States, she departed from the common truth of history, as it respected their lot in life, when she condemned her Uncle Tom to his tragical fate. For it was not the *character* of Uncle Tom that she greatly idealized, as has been so

Uncle Tom at Home

often asserted ; it was the category of events that were made to befall him.

As citizens of the American Republic, these old negroes—now known as "colored gentlemen," surrounded by "colored ladies and gentlemen"—have not done a great deal. The bud of liberty was ingrafted too late on the ancient slave-stock to bear much fruit. But they are interesting, as contemporaries of a type of Kentucky negro whose virtues and whose sorrows, dramatically embodied in literature, have become a by-word throughout the civilized world. And now that the war-cloud is lifting from over the landscape of the past, so that it lies still clear to the eyes of those who were once the dwellers amid its scenes, it is perhaps a good time to scan it and note some of its great moral landmarks before it grows remoter and is finally forgotten.

II

THESE three types—Mrs. Stowe's Uncle Tom, and the Shelbys, his master and mistress — were the outgrowth of natural and historic conditions peculiar to Kentucky. "Perhaps," wrote Mrs. Stowe in her novel, "the mildest form of the system of slavery is to be seen in the State of Kentucky. The general prevalence of agricultural pursuits of a quiet and gradual nature, not requiring those periodic seasons of hurry and pressure that are called for in the business of more southern districts, makes the task of the negro a more healthful and reasonable one; while the master, content with a more gradual style of acquisition, had not those temptations to hard-heartedness which always overcome frail human nature when the prospect of sudden and rapid gain is weighed in the balance with no heavier counterpoise than the interests of the helpless and unprotected." These words contain many truths.

Uncle Tom at Home

For it must not be forgotten, first of all, that the condition of the slave in Kentucky was measurably determined by certain physical laws which lay beyond the control of the most inhuman master. Consider the nature of the country—elevated, rolling, without miasmatic districts or fatal swamps; the soil in the main slave-holding portions of the State easily tilled, abundantly yielding; the climate temperate and invigorating. Consider the system of agriculture — not that of vast plantations, but of small farms, part of which regularly consisted of woodland and meadow that required little attention. Consider the further limitations to this system imposed by the range of the great Kentucky staples—it being in the nature of corn, wheat, hemp, and tobacco, not to yield profits sufficient to justify the employment of an immense predial force, nor to require seasons of forced and exhausting labor. It is evident that under such conditions slavery was not stamped with those sadder features which it wore beneath a devastating sun, amid unhealthy or sterile regions of country, and through the herding together of hundreds of slaves who had the outward but not the inward discipline of an army. True, one recalls here the often quoted words of Jefferson on the raising of tobacco—words nearly as often mis-

Uncle Tom at Home

applied as quoted; for he was considering the condition of slaves who were unmercifully worked on exhausted lands by a certain proletarian type of master, who did not feed and clothe them. Only under such circumstances could the culture of this plant be described as "productive of infinite wretchedness," and those engaged in it as "in a continual state of exertion beyond the powers of nature to support." It was by reason of these physical facts that slavery in Kentucky assumed the phase which is to be distinguished as domestic; and it was this mode that had prevailed at the North and made emancipation easy.

Furthermore, in all history the condition of an enslaved race under the enslaving one has been partly determined by the degree of moral justification with which the latter has regarded the subject of human bondage; and the life of the Kentucky negro, say in the days of Uncle Tom, was further modified by the body of laws which had crystallized as the sentiment of the people, slave-holders themselves. But even these laws were only a partial exponent of what that sentiment was; for some of the severest were practically a dead letter, and the clemency of the negro's treatment by the prevailing type of master made amends for the hard provisions of others.

Uncle Tom at Home

It would be a difficult thing to write the history of slavery in Kentucky. It is impossible to write a single page of it here. But it may be said that the conscience of the great body of the people was always sensitive touching the rightfulness of the institution. At the very outset it seems to have been recognized simply for the reason that the early settlers were emigrants from slave-holding States and brought their negroes with them. The commonwealth began its legislation on the subject in the face of an opposing sentiment. By early statute restriction was placed on the importation of slaves, and from the first they began to be emancipated. Throughout the seventy-five years of pro-slavery State life, the general conscience was always troubled.

The churches took up the matter. Great preachers, whose names were influential beyond the State, denounced the system from the pulpit, pleaded for the humane and Christian treatment of slaves, advocated gradual emancipation. One religious body after another proclaimed the moral evil of it, and urged that the young be taught and prepared as soon as possible for freedom. Antislavery publications and addresses, together with the bold words of great political leaders, acted as a further leaven

Uncle Tom at Home

in the mind of the slave-holding class. As evidence of this, when the new constitution of the State was to be adopted, about 1850, thirty thousand votes were cast in favor of an open clause in it, whereby gradual emancipation should become a law as soon as the majority of the citizens should deem it expedient for the peace of society; and these votes represented the richest, most intelligent slave-holders in the State.

In general the laws were perhaps the mildest. Some it is vital to the subject not to pass over. If slaves were inhumanly treated by their owner or not supplied with proper food and clothing, they could be taken from him and sold to a better master. This law was not inoperative. I have in mind the instance of a family who lost their negroes in this way, were socially disgraced, and left their neighborhood. If the owner of a slave had bought him on condition of not selling him out of the county, or into the Southern States, or so as not to separate him from his family, he could be sued for violation of contract. This law shows the opposition of the better class of Kentucky masters to the slave-trade, and their peculiar regard for the family ties of their negroes. In the earliest Kentucky newspapers will be found advertisements of the sales of negroes, on condition that

Uncle Tom at Home

they would be bought and kept within the county or the State. It was within chancery jurisdiction to prevent the separation of families. The case may be mentioned of a master who was tried by his Church for unnecessarily separating a husband from his wife. Sometimes slaves who had been liberated and had gone to Canada voluntarily returned into service under their former masters. Lest these should be overreached, they were to be taken aside and examined by the court to see that they understood the consequences of their own action, and were free from improper constraint. On the other hand, if a slave had a right to his freedom, he could file a bill in chancery and enforce his master's assent thereto.

But a clear distinction must be made between the mild view entertained by the Kentucky slave-holders regarding the system itself and their dislike of the agitators of forcible and immediate emancipation. A community of masters, themselves humane to their negroes and probably intending to liberate them in the end, would yet combine into a mob to put down individual or organized antislavery efforts, because they resented what they regarded as interference of the abolitionist with their own affairs, and believed his measures inexpedient

Uncle Tom at Home

for the peace of society. Therefore, the history of the antislavery movement in Kentucky, at times so turbulent, must not be used to show the sentiment of the people regarding slavery itself.

III

FROM these general considerations it is possible to enter more closely upon a study of the domestic life and relations of Uncle Tom and the Shelbys.

"Whoever visits some estates there," wrote Mrs. Stowe, "and witnesses the good-humored indulgence of some masters and mistresses and the affectionate loyalty of some slaves, might be tempted to dream of the oft-fabled poetic legend of a patriarchal institution." Along with these words, taken from *Uncle Tom's Cabin*, I should like to quote an extract from a letter written me by Mrs. Stowe under date of April 30, 1886:

"In relation to your letter, I would say that I never lived in Kentucky, but spent many years in Cincinnati, which is separated from Kentucky only by the Ohio River, which, as a shrewd politician remarked, was dry one-half the year and frozen the other. My father was president of a theological seminary at Walnut Hills, near Cincinnati, and with him I travelled and

THE MAMMY

Uncle Tom at Home

visited somewhat extensively in Kentucky, and there became acquainted with those excellent slave-holders delineated in *Uncle Tom's Cabin*. I saw many counterparts of the Shelbys—people humane, conscientious, just and generous, who regarded slavery as an evil and were anxiously considering their duties to the slave. But it was not till I had finally left the West, and my husband was settled as professor in Bowdoin College, Brunswick, Maine, that the passage of the fugitive-slave law and the distresses that followed it drew this from me."

The typical boy on a Kentucky farm was tenderly associated from infancy with the negroes of the household and the fields. His old black "Mammy" became almost his first mother, and was but slowly crowded out of his conscience and his heart by the growing image of the true one. She had perhaps nursed him at her bosom when he was not long enough to stretch across it, sung over his cradle at noon and at midnight, taken him out upon the velvety grass beneath the shade of the elm-trees to watch his first manly resolution of standing alone in the world and walking the vast distance of some inches. Often, in boyish years, when flying from the house with a loud appeal from the incomprehensible code of Anglo-Saxon punishment for small misdemeanors, he had run to those black arms and cried himself to sleep in the lap of

Uncle Tom at Home

African sympathy. As he grew older, alas! his first love grew faithless; and while "Mammy" was good enough in her way and sphere, his wandering affections settled humbly at the feet of another great functionary of the household —the cook in the kitchen. To him her keys were as the keys to the kingdom of heaven, for his immortal soul was his immortal appetite. When he stood by the biscuit bench while she, pausing amid the varied industries that went into the preparation of an old-time Kentucky supper, made him marvellous geese of dough, with farinaceous feathers and genuine coffee-grains for eyes, there was to him no other artist in the world who possessed the secret of so commingling the useful with the beautiful.

The little half-naked imps, too, playing in the dirt like glossy blackbirds taking a bath of dust, were his sweetest, because perhaps his forbidden, companions. With them he went clandestinely to the fatal duck-pond in the stable lot, to learn the art of swimming on a walnut rail. With them he raced up and down the lane on blooded alder-stalk horses, afterwards leading the exhausted coursers into stables of green bushes and haltering them high with a cotton string. It was one of these hatless children of original Guinea that had crept up to him as he lay asleep in the summer grass

Uncle Tom at Home

and told him where the best hidden of all nests was to be found in a far fence corner—that of the high-tempered, scolding guinea-hen. To them he showed his first Barlow knife; for them he blew his first home-made whistle. He is their petty tyrant to-day; to-morrow he will be their repentant friend, dividing with them his marbles and proposing a game of hop-scotch. Upon his dialect, his disposition, his whole character, is laid the ineffaceable impress of theirs, so that they pass into the final reckoning-up of his life here and in the world to come.

But Uncle Tom!—the negro overseer of the place—the greatest of all the negroes—greater even than the cook, when one is not hungry. How often has he straddled Uncle Tom's neck, or ridden behind him afield on a barebacked horse to the jingling music of the trace-chains! It is Uncle Tom who plaits his hempen whip and ties the cracker in a knot that will stay. It is Uncle Tom who brings him his first young squirrel to tame, the teeth of which are soon to be planted in his right forefinger. Many a time he slips out of the house to take his dinner or supper in the cabin with Uncle Tom; and during long winter evenings he loves to sit before those great roaring cabin fireplaces that throw their red and yellow lights over the

Uncle Tom at Home

half circle of black faces and on the mysteries of broom-making, chair-bottoming, and the cobbling of shoes. Like the child who listens to "Uncle Remus," he, too, hears songs and stories, and creeps back to the house with a wondering look in his eyes and a vague hush of spirit.

Then come school-days and vacations, during which, as Mrs. Stowe says, he may teach Uncle Tom to make his letters on a slate or expound to him the Scriptures. Then, too, come early adventures with the gun, and 'coon hunts and 'possum hunts with the negroes under the round moon, with the long-eared, deep-voiced hounds—to him delicious and ever-memorable nights! The crisp air, through which the breath rises like white incense, the thick autumn leaves, begemmed with frost, rustling underfoot; the shadows of the mighty trees; the strained ear; the heart leaping with excitement; the negroes and dogs mingling their wild delight in music that wakes the echoes of distant hill-sides. Away! Away! mile after mile, hour after hour, to where the purple and golden persimmons hang low from the boughs, or where from topmost limbs the wild grape drops its countless clusters in a black cascade a sheer two hundred feet.

Now he is a boy no longer, but has his first

Uncle Tom at Home

love-affair, which sends a thrill through all those susceptible cabins; has his courtship, which gives rise to many a wink and innuendo; and brings home his bride, whose coming converts every youngster into a living rolling ball on the ground, and opens the feasts and festivities of universal joy.

Then some day "ole Marster" dies, and the negroes, one by one, young and old, file into the darkened parlor to take a last look at his quiet face. He had his furious temper, "ole Marster" had, and his sins — which God forgive! To-day he will be buried, and to-morrow "young Marster" will inherit his saddle-horse and ride out into the fields.

Thus he has come into possession of his negroes. Among them are a few whose working days are over. These are to be kindly cared for, decently buried. Next are the active laborers, and, last, the generation of children. He knows them all by name, capacity, and disposition; is bound to them by live-long associations; hears their communications and complaints. When he goes to town, he is charged with commissions, makes purchases with their own money. Continuing the course of his father, he sets about making them capable, contented workmen. There shall be special training for special aptitude. One shall be

Uncle Tom at Home

made a blacksmith, a second a carpenter, a third a cobbler of shoes. In all the general industries of the farm, education shall not be lacking. It is claimed that a Kentucky negro invented the hemp-brake. As a result of this effective management, the Southern planter, looking northward, will pay him a handsome premium for his blue-grass slave. He will have no white overseer. He does not like the type of man. Besides, one is not needed. Uncle Tom served his father in this capacity; let him be.

Among his negroes he finds a bad one. What shall he do with him? Keep him? Keeping him makes him worse, and, moreover, he corrupts the others. Set him free? That is to put a reward upon evil. Sell him to his neighbors? They do not want him. If they did, he would not sell him to them. He sells him into the South. This is a statement, not an apology. Here, for a moment, one touches the terrible subject of the internal slave-trade. Negroes were sold from Kentucky into the Southern market because, as has just been said, they were bad, or by reason of the law of partible inheritance, or, as was the case with Mrs. Stowe's Uncle Tom, under constraint of debt. Of course, in many cases, they were sold wantonly and cruelly; but these, however

THE COOK

Uncle Tom at Home

many, were not enough to make the internal slave-trade more than an incidental and subordinate feature of the system. The belief that negroes in Kentucky were regularly bred and reared for the Southern market is a mistaken one. Mrs. Stowe herself fell into the error of basing an argument for the prevalence of the slave-trade in this State upon the notion of exhausted lands, as the following passage from *The Key to Uncle Tom's Cabin* shows:

" In Delaware, Maryland, Virginia, and Kentucky slave-labor long ago impoverished the soil almost beyond recovery and became entirely unprofitable."

Those words were written some thirty-five years ago and refer to a time long prior to that date. Now, the fact is that at least one-half the soil of Kentucky has never been under cultivation, and could not, therefore, have been exhausted by slave-labor. At least a half of the remainder, though cultivated ever since, is still not seriously exhausted; and of the small portion still left a large share was always naturally poor, so that for this reason slave-labor was but little employed on it. The great slave-holding region of the State was the fertile region which has never been impoverished. To return from this digression, it may be well that the typical Kentucky

Uncle Tom at Home

farmer does not find among his negroes a bad one; for in consequence of the early non-importation of slaves for barter or sale, and through long association with the household, they have been greatly elevated and humanized. If he must sell a good one, he will seek a buyer among his neighbors. He will even ask the negro to name his choice of a master and try to consummate his wish. No purchaser near by, he will mount his saddle-horse and look for one in the adjoining county. In this way the negroes of different estates and neighborhoods were commonly connected by kinship and intermarriage. How unjust to say that such a master did not feel affection for his slaves, anxiety for their happiness, sympathy with the evils inseparable from their condition. Let me cite the case of a Kentucky master who had failed. He could pay his debts by sacrificing his negroes or his farm, one or the other. To avoid separating the former, probably sending some of them South, he kept them in a body and sold his farm. Any one who knows the Kentuckian's love of land and home will know what this means. A few years, and the war left him without anything. Another case is more interesting still. A master having failed, actually hurried his negroes off to Canada. Tried for defrauding his creditors,

Uncle Tom at Home

and that by slave-holding jurors, he was acquitted. The plea of his counsel, among other arguments, was the master's unwillingness to see his old and faithful servitors scattered and suffering. After emancipation old farm hands sometimes refused to budge from their cabins. Their former masters paid them for their services as long as they could work, and supported them when helpless. I have in mind an instance where a man, having left Kentucky, sent back hundreds of dollars to an aged, needy domestic, though himself far from rich; and another case where a man still contributes annually to the maintenance of those who ceased to work for him the quarter of a century ago.

The good in human nature is irrepressible. Slavery, evil as it was, when looked at from the remoteness of human history as it is to be, will be adjudged an institution that gave development to certain noble types of character. Along with other social forces peculiar to the age, it produced in Kentucky a kind of farmer, the like of which will never appear again. He had the aristocratic virtues: highest notions of personal liberty and personal honor, a fine especial scorn of anything that was mean, little, cowardly. As an agriculturist he was not driving or merciless or grasping; the rapid amassing of wealth was not among his pas-

Uncle Tom at Home

sions, the contention of splendid living not among his thorns. To a certain carelessness of riches he added a certain profuseness of expenditure; and indulgent towards his own pleasures, towards others, his equals or dependents, he bore himself with a spirit of kindness and magnanimity. Intolerant of tyranny, he was no tyrant. To say of such a man, as Jefferson said of every slave-holder, that he lived in perpetual exercise of the most boisterous passions and unremitting despotism, and in the exaction of the most degrading submission, was to pronounce judgment hasty and unfair. Rather did Mrs. Stowe, while not blind to his faults, discern his virtues when she made him, embarrassed by debt, exclaim: "If anybody had said to me that I should sell Tom down South to one of those rascally traders, I should have said, 'Is thy servant a dog that he should do this thing?'"

IV

BUT there was another person who, more than the master, sustained close relationship to the negro life of the household — the mistress. In the person of Mrs. Shelby, Mrs. Stowe described some of the best traits of a Kentucky woman of the time; but perhaps only a Southern woman herself could do full justice to a character which many duties and many burdens endued with extraordinary strength and varied efficiency.

She was mistress of distinct realms — the house and the cabins—and the guardian of the bonds between the two, which were always troublesome, often delicate, sometimes distressing. In those cabins were nearly always some poor creatures needing sympathy and watch-care: the superannuated mothers helpless with babes, babes helpless without mothers, the sick, perhaps the idiotic. Apparel must be had for all. Standing in her doorway and pointing to the meadow, she must be able to say in the

Uncle Tom at Home

words of a housewife of the period, " There are the sheep ; now get your clothes." Some must be taught to keep the spindle and the loom going ; others trained for dairy, laundry, kitchen, dining-room ; others yet taught fine needlework. Upon her fell the labor of private instruction and moral exhortation, for the teaching of negroes was not forbidden in Kentucky.

She must remind them that their marriage vows are holy and binding ; must interpose between mothers and their cruel punishment of their own offspring. Hardest of all, she must herself punish for lying, theft, immorality. Her own children must be guarded against temptation and corrupting influences. In her life no cessation of this care year in and year out. Beneath every other trouble the secret conviction that she has no right to enslave these creatures, and that, however improved their condition, their life is one of great and necessary evils. Mrs. Stowe well makes her say : "I have tried—tried most faithfully as a Christian woman should—to do my duty towards these poor, simple, dependent creatures. I have cared for them, instructed them, watched over them, and known all their little cares and joys for years. . . . I have taught them the duties of the family, of parent and child, and husband and wife. . . . I thought, by kindness and care and instruction,

Uncle Tom at Home

I could make the condition of mine better than freedom." Sorely overburdened and heroic mould of woman! Fulfilling each day a round of intricate duties, rising at any hour of the night to give medicine to the sick, liable at any time, in addition to the cares of her great household, to see an entire family of acquaintances arriving unannounced, with trunks and servants of their own, for a visit protracted in accordance with the large hospitalities of the time. What wonder if, from sheer inability to do all things herself, she trains her negroes to different posts of honor, so that the black cook finally expels her from her own kitchen and rules over that realm as an autocrat of unquestioned prerogatives?

Mistresses of this kind had material reward in the trusty adherence of their servants during the war. Their relations throughout this period—so well calculated to try the loyalty of the African nature—would of themselves make up a volume of the most touching incidents. Even to-day one will find in many Kentucky households survivals of the old order—find "Aunt Chloe" ruling as a despot in the kitchen, and making her will the pivotal point of the whole domestic system. I have spent nights with a young Kentuckian, self-willed and high-spirited, whose occasional refusals to rise for a

Uncle Tom at Home

half-past five o'clock breakfast always brought the cook from the kitchen up to his bedroom, where she delivered her commands in a voice worthy of Catherine the Great. "We shall have to get up," he would say, "or there'll be a row!" One may yet see old negresses setting out for an annual or a semi-annual visit to their former mistresses, and bearing some offering—a basket of fruits or flowers. I should like to mention the case of one who died after the war and left her two children to her mistress, to be reared and educated. The troublesome, expensive charge was faithfully executed.

Here, in the hard realities of daily life, here is where the crushing burden of slavery fell—on the women of the South. History has yet to do justice to the noblest type of them, whether in Kentucky or elsewhere. In view of what they accomplished, despite the difficulties in their way, there is nothing they have found harder to forgive in the women of the North than the failure to sympathize with them in the struggles and sorrows of their lot, and to realize that *they* were the real practical philanthropists of the negro race.

V

BUT as is the master, so is the slave, and it is through the characters of the Shelbys that we must approach that of Uncle Tom. For of all races, the African—superstitious, indolent, singing, dancing, impressionable creature—depends upon others for enlightenment, training, and happiness. If, therefore, you find him so intelligent that he may be sent on important business, so honest that he may be trusted with money, house, and home, so loyal that he will not seize opportunity to become free; if you find him endowed with the manly virtues of dignity and self-respect united to the Christian virtues of humility, long-suffering, and forgiveness, then do not, in marvelling at him on these accounts, quite forget his master and his mistress—they made him what he was. And it is something to be said on their behalf, that in their household was developed a type of slave that could be set upon a sublime moral pinnacle to attract the admiration of the world.

Uncle Tom at Home

Attention is fixed on Uncle Tom first as head-servant of the farm. In a small work on slavery in Kentucky by George Harris, it is stated that masters chose the cruelest of their negroes for this office. It is not true, exceptions allowed for. The work would not be worth mentioning, had not so many people at the North believed it. The amusing thing is, they believed Mrs. Stowe also. But if Mrs. Stowe's account of slavery in Kentucky is true, Harris's is not.

It is true that Uncle Tom inspired the other negroes with some degree of fear. He was censor of morals, and reported derelictions of the lazy, the destructive, and the thievish. For instance, an Uncle Tom on one occasion told his master of the stealing of a keg of lard, naming the thief and the hiding-place. "Say not a word about it," replied his master. The next day he rode out into the field where the culprit was ploughing, and, getting down, walked along beside him. "What's the matter, William?" he asked, after a while; "you can't look me in the face as usual." William burst into tears, and confessed everything. "Come to-night, and I will arrange so that you can put the lard back and nobody will ever know you took it." The only punishment was a little moral teaching; but the

Uncle Tom at Home

Uncle Tom in the case, though he kept his secret, looked for some days as though the dignity of his office had not been suitably upheld by his master.

It was Uncle Tom's duty to get the others off to work in the morning. In the fields he did not drive the work, but led it — being a master-workman — led the cradles and the reaping-hooks, the hemp-breaking and the corn-shucking. The spirit of happy music went with the workers. They were not goaded through their daily tasks by the spur of pitiless husbandry. Nothing was more common than their voluntary contests of skill and power. My recollection reaches only to the last two or three years of slavery; but I remember the excitement with which I witnessed some of these hard-fought battles of the negroes. Rival hemp-breakers of the neighborhood, meeting in the same field, would slip out long before breakfast and sometimes never stop for dinner. So it was with cradling, corn-shucking, or corn-cutting — in all work where rivalries were possible. No doubt there were other motives. So much work was a day's task; for more there was extra pay. A capital hand, by often performing double or treble the required amount, would clear a neat profit in a season. The days of severest

Uncle Tom at Home

labor fell naturally in harvest-time. But then intervals of rest in the shade were commonly given; and milk, coffee, or, when the prejudice of the master did not prevent (which was not often), whiskey was distributed between mealtimes. As a rule, they worked without hurry. De Tocqueville gave unintentional testimony to characteristic slavery in Kentucky when he described the negroes as "loitering" in the fields. On one occasion the hands dropped work to run after a rabbit the dogs had started. A passer-by indignantly reported the fact to the master. "Sir," said the old gentleman, with a hot face, "I'd have whipped the last d—n rascal of 'em if they *hadn't* run 'im!"

The negroes made money off their truck-patches, in which they raised melons, broom-corn, vegetables. When Charles Sumner was in Kentucky, he saw with almost incredulous eyes the comfortable cabins with their flowers and poultry, the fruitful truck-patches, and a genuine Uncle Tom—"a black gentleman with his own watch!" Well enough does Mrs. Stowe put these words into her hero's mouth, when he hears he is to be sold: "I'm feared things will be kinder goin' to rack when I'm gone. Mas'r can't be 'spected to be a-pryin' round everywhere as I've done, a-keepin' up all the

Uncle Tom at Home

ends. The boys means well, but they's powerful car'less."

More interesting is Uncle Tom's character as a preacher. Contemporary with him in Kentucky was a class of men among his people who exhorted, held prayer-meetings in the cabins and baptizings in the woods, performed marriage ceremonies, and enjoyed great freedom of movement. There was one in nearly every neighborhood, and together they wrought effectively in the moral development of their race. I have nothing to say here touching the vast and sublime conception which Mrs. Stowe formed of "Uncle Tom's" spiritual nature. But no idealized manifestation of it is better than this simple occurrence: One of these negro preachers was allowed by his master to fill a distant appointment. Belated once, and returning home after the hour forbidden for slaves to be abroad, he was caught by the patrol and cruelly whipped. As the blows fell, his only words were: "Jesus Christ suffered for righteousness' sake; so kin I." Another of them was recommended for deacon's orders and actually ordained. When liberty came, he refused to be free, and continued to work in his master's family till his death. With considerable knowledge of the Bible and a fluent tongue, he would nevertheless sometimes grow

Uncle Tom at Home

confused while preaching and lose his train of thought. At these embarrassing junctures it was his wont suddenly to call out at the top of his voice, "Saul! Saul! why persecutest thou me?" The effect upon his hearers was electrifying; and as none but a very highly favored being could be thought worthy of enjoying this persecution, he thus converted his loss of mind into spiritual reputation. A third, named Peter Cotton, united the vocations of exhorter and wood-chopper. He united them literally, for one moment Peter might be seen standing on his log chopping away, and the next kneeling down beside it praying. He got his mistress to make him a long jeans coat and on the ample tails of it to embroider, by his direction, sundry texts of Scripture, such as: "Come unto me, all ye that are heavy laden!" Thus literally clothed with righteousness, Peter went from cabin to cabin preaching the Word. Well for him if that other Peter could have seen him.

These men sometimes made a pathetic addition to their marriage ceremonies: "Until death or *our higher powers* do you separate!"

Another typical contemporary of Uncle Tom's was the negro fiddler. It should be remembered that before he hears he is to be sold South, Uncle Tom is pictured as a light-heart-

THE PREACHER

Uncle Tom at Home

ed creature, capering and dancing in his cabin. There was no lack of music in those cabins. The banjo was played, but more commonly the fiddle. A home-made variety of the former consisted of a crook-necked, hard-shell gourd and a piece of sheepskin. There were sometimes other instruments—the flageolet and the triangle. I have heard of a kettle-drum's being made of a copper still. A Kentucky negro carried through the war as a tambourine the skull of a mule, the rattling teeth being secured in the jawbones. Of course bones were everywhere used. Negro music on one or more instruments was in the highest vogue at the house of the master. The young Kentuckians often used it on serenading bravuras. The old fiddler, most of all, was held in reverent esteem and met with the gracious treatment of the minstrel in feudal halls. At parties and weddings, at picnics in the summer woods, he was the soul of melody; and with an eye to the high demands upon his art, he widened his range of selections and perfected according to native standards his inimitable technique. The deep, tender, pure feeling in the song "Old Kentucky Home" is a true historic interpretation.

It is wide of the mark to suppose that on such a farm as that of the Shelbys, the negroes

Uncle Tom at Home

were in a perpetual frenzy of discontent or felt any burning desire for freedom. It is difficult to reach a true general conclusion on this delicate subject. But it must go for something that even the Kentucky abolitionists of those days will tell you that well-treated negroes cared not a snap for liberty. Negroes themselves, and very intelligent ones, will give you to-day the same assurance. It is an awkward discovery to make, that some of them still cherish resentment towards agitators who came secretly among them, fomented discontent, and led them away from homes to which they afterwards returned. And I want to state here, for no other reason than that of making an historic contribution to the study of the human mind and passions, that a man's views of slavery in those days did not determine his treatment of his own slaves. The only case of mutiny and stampede that I have been able to discover in a certain part of Kentucky, took place among the negroes of a man who was known as an outspoken emancipationist. He pleaded for the freedom of the negro, but in the mean time worked him at home with the chain round his neck and the ball resting on his plough.

Christmas was, of course, the time of holiday merrymaking, and the "Ketchin' marster an' mistiss Christmus gif'" was a great feature.

Uncle Tom at Home

One morning an aged couple presented themselves.

"Well, what do you want for your Christmas gift?"

"Freedom, mistiss!"

"Freedom! Haven't you been as good as free for the last ten years?"

"Yaas, mistiss; but—freedom mighty sweet!"

"Then take your freedom!"

The only method of celebrating the boon was the moving into a cabin on the neighboring farm of their mistress's aunt and being freely supported there as they had been freely supported at home.

Mrs. Stowe has said, "There is nothing picturesque or beautiful in the family attachment of old servants, which is not to be found in countries where these servants are legally free." On the contrary, a volume of incidents might readily be gathered, the picturesqueness and beauty of which are due wholly to the fact that the negroes were not free, but slaves. Indeed, many could never have happened at all but in this relationship. I cite the case of an old negro who was buying his freedom from his master, who continued to make payments during the war, and made the final one at the time of General Kirby Smith's invasion of Kentucky. After he had paid him the uttermost farthing,

Uncle Tom at Home

he told him that if he should ever be a slave again, he wanted him for his master. Take the case of an old negress who had been allowed to accumulate considerable property. At her death she willed it to her young master instead of to her sons, as she would have been allowed to do. But the war! what is to be said of the part the negro took in that? Is there in the drama of humanity a figure more picturesque or more pathetic than the figure of the African slave, as he followed his master to the battle-field, marched and hungered and thirsted with him, served and cheered and nursed him—that master who was fighting to keep him in slavery? Instances are too many; but the one may be mentioned of a Kentucky negro who followed his young master into the Southern army, stayed with him till he fell on the field, lay hid out in the bushes a week, and finally, after a long time and many hardships, got back to his mistress in Kentucky, bringing his dead master's horse and purse and trinkets. This subject comprises a whole vast field of its own; and if the history of it is ever written, it will be written in the literature of the South, for there alone lies the knowledge and *the love.*

It is only through a clear view of the peculiar features of slavery in Kentucky before the war that one can understand the general status of

Uncle Tom at Home

the negroes of Kentucky at the present time. Perhaps in no other State has the race made less endeavor to push itself into equality with the white. This fact must be explained as in part resulting from the conservative ideals of Kentucky life in general. But it is more largely due to the influences of a system which, though no longer in vogue, is still remembered, still powerful to rule the minds of a naturally submissive and susceptible people. The kind, affectionate relations of the races under the old regime have continued with so little interruption that the blacks remain content with their inferiority, and lazily drift through life. I venture to make the statement that, wherever in the United States they have attempted most to enforce their new-born rights, they have either, on the one hand, been encouraged to do so, or have, on the other, been driven to self-assertion by harsh treatment. But treated always kindly, always as hopelessly inferior beings, they will do least for themselves. This, it is believed, is the key-note to the situation in Kentucky at the present time.

COUNTY COURT DAY IN KENTUCKY

I

THE institutions of the Kentuckian have deep root in his rich social nature. He loves the swarm. The very motto of the State is a declaration of good-fellowship, and the seal of the commonwealth the act of shaking hands. Divided, he falls. The Kentuckian must be one of many; must assert himself, not through the solitary exercise of his intellect, but the senses; must see men about him who are fat; grip his friend, hear cordial, hearty conversation, realize the play of his emotions. Society is the multiple of himself.

Hence his fondness for large gatherings: open-air assemblies of the democratic sort—great agricultural fairs, race-courses, political meetings, barbecues and burgoos in the woods—where no one is pushed to the wall, or reduced to a seat and to silence, where all may move about at will, seek and be sought, make and receive impressions. Quiet masses of people in-doors absorb him less. He is not fond of

County Court Day in Kentucky

lectures, does not build splendid theatres or expend lavishly for opera, is almost of Puritan excellence in the virtue of church-going, which in the country is attended with neighborly reunions.

This large social disposition underlies the history of the most social of all his days—a day that has long had its observance embedded in the structure of his law, is invested with the authority and charm of old-time usage and reminiscence, and still enables him to commingle business and pleasure in a way of his own. Hardly more characteristic of the Athenian was the agora, or the forum of the Roman, than is county court day characteristic of the Kentuckian. In the open square around the court-house of the county-seat he has had the centre of his public social life, the arena of his passions and amusements, the rallying-point of his political discussions, the market-place of his business transactions, the civil unit of his institutional history.

It may be that some stranger has sojourned long enough in Kentucky to have grown familiar with the wonted aspects of a county town. He has remarked the easy swing of its daily life : amicable groups of men sitting around the front entrances of the hotels ; the few purchasers and promenaders on the uneven brick

County Court Day in Kentucky

pavements ; the few vehicles of draught and carriage scattered along the level white thoroughfares. All day the subdued murmur of patient local traffic has scarcely drowned the twittering of English sparrows in the maples. Then comes a Monday morning when the whole scene changes. The world has not been dead, but only sleeping. Wnence this sudden surging crowd of rural folk—these lowing herds in the streets? Is it some animated pastoral come to town? some joyful public anniversary? some survival in altered guise of the English country fair of mellower times? or a vision of what the little place will be a century hence, when American life shall be packed and agitated and tense all over the land? What a world of homogeneous, good-looking, substantial, reposeful people with honest front and amiable meaning! What bargaining and buying and selling by ever-forming, ever-dissolving groups, with quiet laughter and familiar talk and endless interchange of domestic interrogatories! You descend into the street to study the doings and spectacles from a nearer approach, and stop to ask the meaning of it. Ah! it is county court day in Kentucky ; it is the Kentuckians in the market-place.

II

THEY have been assembling here now for nearly a hundred years. One of the first demands of the young commonwealth in the woods was that its vigorous, passionate life should be regulated by the usages of civil law. Its monthly county courts, with justices of the peace, were derived from the Virginia system of jurisprudence, where they formed the aristocratic feature of the government. Virginia itself owed these models to England; and thus the influence of the courts and of the decent and orderly yeomanry of both lands passed, as was singularly fitting, over into the ideals of justice erected by the pure-blooded colony. As the town-meeting of Boston town perpetuated the folkmote of the Anglo-Saxon free state, and the Dutch village communities on the shores of the Hudson revived the older ones on the banks of the Rhine, so in Kentucky, through Virginia, there were transplanted by the people, themselves of clean stock and

County Court Day in Kentucky

with strong conservative ancestral traits, the influences and elements of English law in relation to the county, the court, and the justice of the peace.

Through all the old time of Kentucky State life there towers up the figure of the justice of the peace. Commissioned by the Governor to hold monthly court, he had not always a court-house wherein to sit, but must buy land in the midst of a settlement or town whereon to build one, and build also the contiguous necessity of civilization—a jail. In the rude court-room he had a long platform erected, usually running its whole width; on this platform he had a ruder wooden bench placed, likewise extending all the way across; and on this bench, having ridden into town, it may be, in dun-colored leggings, broadcloth pantaloons, a pigeon-tailed coat, a shingle-caped overcoat, and a twelve-dollar high fur hat, he sat gravely and sturdily down amid his peers; looking out upon the bar, ranged along a wooden bench beneath, and prepared to consider the legal needs of his assembled neighbors. Among them all the very best was he; chosen for age, wisdom, means, weight and probity of character; as a rule, not profoundly versed in the law, perhaps knowing nothing of it—being a Revolutionary soldier, a pioneer, or a farmer—but endowed

County Court Day in Kentucky

with a sure, robust common-sense and rectitude of spirit that enabled him to divine what the law was; shaking himself fiercely loose from the grip of mere technicalities, and deciding by the natural justice of the case; giving decisions of equal authority with the highest court, an appeal being rarely taken; perpetuating his own authority by appointing his own associates: with all his shortcomings and weaknesses a notable, historic figure, high-minded, fearless, and incorruptible, dignified, patient, and strong, and making the county court days of Kentucky for wellnigh half a century memorable to those who have lived to see justice less economically and less honorably administered.

But besides the legal character and intent of the day which was thus its first and dominant feature, divers things drew the folk together. Even the justice himself may have had quite other than magisterial reasons for coming to town; certainly the people had. They must interchange opinions about local and national politics, observe the workings of their own laws, pay and contract debts, acquire and transfer property, discuss all questions relative to the welfare of the community—holding, in fact, a county court day much like one in Virginia in the middle of the seventeenth century.

III

BUT after business was over, time hung idly on their hands; and being vigorous men, hardened by work in forest and field, trained in foot and limb to fleetness and endurance, and fired with admiration of physical prowess, like riotous school-boys out on a half-holiday, they fell to playing. All through the first quarter of the century, and for a longer time, county court day in Kentucky was, at least in many parts of the State, the occasion for holding athletic games. The men, young or in the sinewy manhood of more than middle age, assembled once a month at the county-seats to witness and take part in the feats of muscle and courage. They wrestled, threw the sledge, heaved the bar, divided and played at fives, had foot-races for themselves, and quarter-races for their horses. By-and-by, as these contests became a more prominent feature of the day, they would pit against each other the champions of different neighbor-

County Court Day in Kentucky

hoods. It would become widely known beforehand that next county court day "the bully" in one end of the county would whip "the bully" in the other end; so when court day came, and the justices came, and the bullies came, what was the county to do but come also? The crowd repaired to the common, a ring was formed, the little men on the outside who couldn't see, Zaccheus-like, took to the convenient trees, and there was to be seen a fair and square set-to, in which the fist was the battering-ram and the biceps a catapult. What better, more time-honored proof could those backwoods Kentuckians have furnished of the humors in their English blood and of their English pugnacity? But, after all, this was only play, and play never is perfectly satisfying to a man who would rather fight; so from playing they fell to harder work, and throughout this period county court day was the monthly Monday on which the Kentuckian regularly did his fighting. He availed himself liberally of election day, it is true, and of regimental muster in the spring and battalion muster in the fall—great gala occasions; but county court day was by all odds the preferred and highly prized season. It was periodical, and could be relied upon, being written in the law, noted in the almanac, and registered in the heavens.

COURT-HOUSE SQUARE, LEXINGTON, KENTUCKY

County Court Day in Kentucky

A capital day, a most admirable and serene day for fighting. Fights grew like a freshwater polype—by being broken in two : each part produced a progeny. So conventional did the recreation become that difficulties occurring out in the country between times regularly had their settlements postponed until the belligerents could convene with the justices. The men met and fought openly in the streets, the friends of each standing by to see fair play and whet their appetites.

Thus the justices sat quietly on the bench inside, and the people fought quietly in the streets outside, and the day of the month set apart for the conservation of the peace became the approved day for individual war. There is no evidence to be had that either the justices or the constables ever interfered.

These pugilistic encounters had a certain law of beauty : they were affairs of equal combat and of courage. The fight over, animosity was gone, the feud ended. The men must shake hands, go and drink together, become friends. We are touching here upon a grave and curious fact of local history. The fighting habit must be judged by a wholly unique standard. It was the direct outcome of racial traits powerfully developed by social conditions.

IV

ANOTHER noticeable recreation of the day was the drinking. Indeed, the two pleasures went marvellously well together. The drinking led up to the fighting, and the fighting led up to the drinking; and this amiable co-operation might be prolonged at will. The merchants kept barrels of whiskey in their cellars for their customers. Bottles of it sat openly on the counter, half-way between the pocket of the buyer and the shelf of merchandise. There were no saloons separate from the taverns. At these whiskey was sold and drunk without screens or scruples. It was not usually bought by the drink, but by the tickler. The tickler was a bottle of narrow shape, holding a half-pint—just enough to tickle. On a county court day wellnigh a whole town would be tickled. In some parts of the State tables were placed out on the sidewalks, and around these the men sat drinking mint-juleps and playing draw-poker and "old sledge."

THE "TICKLER"

County Court Day in Kentucky

Meantime the day was not wholly given over to playing and fighting and drinking. More and more it was becoming the great public day of the month, and mirroring the life and spirit of the times—on occasion a day of fearful, momentous gravity, as in the midst of war, financial distress, high party feeling; more and more the people gathered together for discussion and the origination of measures determining the events of their history. Gradually new features incrusted it. The politician, observing the crowd, availed himself of it to announce his own candidacy or to wage a friendly campaign, sure, whether popular or unpopular, of a courteous hearing; for this is a virtue of the Kentuckian, to be polite to a public speaker, however little liked his cause. In the spring, there being no fairs, it was the occasion for exhibiting the fine stock of the country, which was led out to some suburban pasture, where the owners made speeches over it. In the winter, at the close of the old or the beginning of the new year, negro slaves were regularly hired out on this day for the ensuing twelvemonth, and sometimes put upon the block before the court-house door and sold for life.

But it was not until near the half of the second quarter of the century that an auctioneer originated stock sales on the open square, and

County Court Day in Kentucky

thus gave to the day the characteristic it has since retained of being the great market-day of the month. Thenceforth its influence was to be more widely felt, to be extended into other counties and even States; thenceforth it was to become more distinctively a local institution without counterpart.

To describe minutely the scenes of a county court day in Kentucky, say at the end of the half-century, would be to write a curious page in the history of the times; for they were possible only through the unique social conditions they portrayed. It was near the most prosperous period of State life under the old regime. The institution of slavery was about to culminate and decline. Agriculture had about as nearly perfected itself as it was ever destined to do under the system of bondage. The war cloud in the sky of the future could be covered with the hand, or at most with the country gentleman's broad-brimmed straw-hat. The whole atmosphere of the times was heavy with ease, and the people, living in perpetual contemplation of their superabundant natural wealth, bore the quality of the land in their manners and dispositions.

When the well-to-do Kentucky farmer got up in the morning, walked out into the porch, stretched himself, and looked at the sun, he

County Court Day in Kentucky

knew that he could summon a sleek, kindly negro to execute every wish and whim—one to search for his misplaced hat, a second to bring him a dipper of ice-water, a third to black his shoes, a fourth to saddle his horse and hitch it at the stiles, a fifth to cook his breakfast, a sixth to wait on him at the table, a seventh to stand on one side and keep off the flies. Breakfast over, he mounted his horse and rode out where "the hands" were at work. The chance was his overseer or negro foreman was there before him: his presence was unnecessary. What a gentleman he was! This was called earning one's bread by the sweat of his brow. *Whose* brow? He yawned. What should he do? One thing he knew he *would* do—take a good nap before dinner. Perhaps he had better ride over to the blacksmith-shop. However, there was nobody there. It was county court day. The sky was blue, the sun golden, the air delightful, the road broad and smooth, the gait of his horse the very poetry of motion. He would go to county court himself. There was really nothing else before him. His wife would want to go, too, and the children.

So away they go, he on horseback or in the family carriage, with black Pompey driving in front and yellow Cæsar riding behind. The turnpike reached, the progress of the family

County Court Day in Kentucky

carriage is interrupted or quite stopped, for there are many other carriages on the road, all going in the same direction. Then pa, growing impatient, orders black Pompey to drive out on one side, whip up the horses, pass the others, and get ahead, so as to escape from the clouds of white limestone dust, which settles thick on the velvet collar of pa's blue cloth coat and in the delicate pink marabou feathers of ma's bonnet: which Pompey can't do, for the faster he goes, the faster the others go, making all the more dust; so that pa gets red in the face, and jumps up in the seat, and looks ready to fight, and thrusts his head out of the window and knocks off his hat; and ma looks nervous, and black Pompey and yellow Cæsar both look white with dust and fear.

A rural cavalcade indeed! Besides the carriages, buggies, horsemen, and pedestrians, there are long droves of stock being hurried on towards the town—hundreds of them. By the time they come together in the town they will be many thousands. For is not this the great stock-market of the West, and does not the whole South look from its rich plantations and cities up to Kentucky for bacon and mules? By-and-by our family carriage does at last get to town, and is left out in the streets along with

County Court Day in Kentucky

many others to block up the passway according to the custom.

The town is packed. It looks as though by some vast suction system it had with one exercise of force drawn all the country life into itself. The poor dumb creatures gathered in from the peaceful fields, and crowded around the court-house, send forth, each after its kind, a general outcry of horror and despair at the tumult of the scene and the unimaginable mystery of their own fate. They overflow into the by-streets, where they take possession of the sidewalks, and debar entrance at private residences. No stock-pens wanted then; none wanted now. If a town legislates against these stock sales on the streets and puts up pens on its outskirts, straightway the stock is taken to some other market, and the town is punished for its airs by a decline in its trade.

As the day draws near noon, the tide of life is at the flood. Mixed in with the tossing horns and nimble heels of the terrified, distressed, half-maddened beasts, are the people. Above the level of these is the discordant choir of shrill-voiced auctioneers on horseback. At the corners of the streets long-haired—and long-eared—doctors in curious hats lecture to eager groups on maladies and philanthropic cures. Every itinerant vender of notion and nostrum

County Court Day in Kentucky

in the country-side is there; every wandering Italian harper or musician of any kind, be he but a sightless fiddler, who brings forth with poor unison of voice and string the brief and too fickle ballads of the time, "Gentle Annie," and "Sweet Alice, Ben Bolt." Strangely contrasted with everything else in physical type and marks of civilization are the mountaineers, who have come down to "the settlemints" driving herds of their lean, stunted cattle, or bringing, in slow-moving, ox-drawn "steamboat" wagons, maple-sugar, and baskets, and poles, and wild mountain fruit—faded wagons, faded beasts, faded clothes, faded faces, faded everything. A general day for buying and selling all over the State. What purchases at the dry-goods stores and groceries to keep all those negroes at home fat and comfortable and comely—cottons, and gay cottonades, and gorgeous turbans, and linseys of prismatic dyes, bags of Rio coffee and barrels of sugar, with many another pleasant thing! All which will not be taken home in the family carriage, but in the wagon which Scipio Africanus is driving in; Scipio, remember; for while the New-Englander has been naming his own flesh and blood Peleg and Hezekiah and Abednego, the Kentuckian has been giving even his negro slaves mighty and classic names, after his taste and

County Court Day in Kentucky

fashion. But very mockingly and satirically do those victorious titles contrast with the condition of those that wear them. A surging populace, an in-town holiday for all rural folk, wholly unlike what may be seen elsewhere in this country. The politician will be sure of his audience to-day in the court-house yard; the seller will be sure of the purchaser; the idle man of meeting one still idler; friend of seeing distant friend; blushing Phyllis, come in to buy fresh ribbons, of being followed through the throng by anxious Corydon.

And what, amid this tumult of life and affairs —what of the justice of the peace, whose figure once towered up so finely? Alas! quite outgrown, pushed aside, and wellnigh forgotten. The very name of the day which once so sternly commemorated the exercise of his authority has wandered into another meaning. "County court day" no longer brings up in the mind the image of the central court-house and the judge on the bench. It is to be greatly feared his noble type is dying. The stain of venality has soiled his homespun ermine, and the trail of the office-seeker passed over his rough-hewn bench. So about this time the new constitution of the commonwealth comes in, to make the autocratic ancient justice over into the modern elective magistrate, and with the end of the

County Court Day in Kentucky

half-century to close a great chapter of wonderful county court days.

But what changes in Kentucky since 1850! How has it fared with the day meantime? What development has it undergone? What contrasts will it show?

Undoubtedly, as seen now, the day is not more interesting by reason of the features it wears than for the sake of comparison with the others it has lost. A singular testimony to the conservative habits of the Kentuckian, and to the stability of his local institutions, is to be found in the fact that it should have come through all this period of upheaval and downfall, of shifting and drifting, and yet remained so much the same. Indeed, it seems in nowise liable to lose its meaning of being the great market and general business day as well as the great social and general laziness day of the month and the State. Perhaps one feature has taken larger prominence—the eager canvassing of voters by local politicians and office-seekers for weeks, sometimes for months, beforehand. Is it not known that even circuit court will adjourn on this day so as to give the clerk and the judge, the bar, the witnesses, an opportunity to hear rival candidates address the assembled crowd? And yet we shall discover differences. These people—these groups of

County Court Day in Kentucky

twos and threes and hundreds, lounging, sitting, squatting, taking every imaginable posture that can secure bodily comfort—are they in any vital sense new Kentuckians in the new South? If you care to understand whether this be true, and what it may mean if it is true, you shall not find a better occasion for doing so than a contemporary county court day.

The Kentuckian nowadays does not come to county court to pick a quarrel or to settle one. He *has* no quarrel. His fist has reverted to its natural use and become a hand. Nor does he go armed. Positively it is true that gentlemen in this State do not now get satisfaction out of each other in the market-place, and that on a modern county court day a three-cornered hat is hardly to be seen. And yet you will go on defining a Kentuckian in terms of his grandfather, unaware that he has changed faster than the family reputation. The fighting habit and the shooting habit were both more than satisfied during the Civil War.

Another old-time feature of the day has disappeared—the open use of the pioneer beverage. Merchants do not now set it out for their customers; in the country no longer is it the law of hospitality to offer it to a guest. To do so would commonly be regarded in the light of as great a liberty as to have omitted it once

County Court Day in Kentucky

would have been considered an offence. The decanter is no longer found on the sideboard in the home; the barrel is not stored in the cellar.

Some features of the old Kentucky marketplace have disappeared. The war and the prostration of the South destroyed that as a market for certain kinds of stock, the raising and sales of which have in consequence declined. Railways have touched the eastern parts of the State, and broken up the distant, toilsome traffic with the steamboat wagons of the mountaineers. No longer is the day the general buying day for the circumjacent country as formerly, when the farmers, having great households of slaves, sent in their wagons and bought on twelve-months' credit, knowing it would be twenty-four months' if they desired. The doctors, too, have nearly vanished from the street corners, though on the highway one may still happen upon the peddler with his pack, and in the midst of an eager throng still may meet the swaying, sightless old fiddler, singing to ears that never tire gay ditties in a cracked and melancholy tone.

Through all changes one feature has remained. It goes back to the most ancient days of local history. The Kentuckian *will* come to county court "to swap horses"; it is

County Court Day in Kentucky

in the blood. In one small town may be seen fifty or a hundred countrymen assembled during the afternoon in a back street to engage in this delightful recreation. Each rides or leads his worst, most objectionable beast; of these, however fair-seeming, none is above suspicion. It is the potter's field, the lazar-house, the beggardom of horse-flesh. The stiff and aged bondsman of the glebe and plough looks out of one filmy eye upon the hopeless wreck of the fleet roadster, and the poor macerated carcass that in days gone by bore its thankless burden over the glistening turnpikes with the speed and softness of the wind has not the strength to return the contemptuous kick which is given him by a lungless, tailless rival. Prices range from nothing upward. Exchanges are made for a piece of tobacco or a watermelon to boot.

But always let us return from back streets and side thoughts to the central court-house square and the general assembly of the people. Go among them; they are not dangerous. Do not use fine words, at which they will prick up their ears uneasily; or delicate sentiments, which will make you less liked; or indulge in flights of thought, which they despise. Remember, here is the dress and the talk and the manners of the street, and fashion yourself

County Court Day in Kentucky

accordingly. Be careful of your speech; men in Kentucky are human. If you can honestly praise them, do so. How they will glow and expand! Censure, and you will get the cold shoulder. For to them praise is friendship and censure enmity. They have wonderful solidarity. Sympathy will on occasion flow through them like an electric current, so that they will soften and melt, or be set on fire. There is a Kentucky sentiment, expending itself in complacent, mellow love of the land, the people, the institutions. You speak to them of the happiness of living in parts of the world where life has infinite variety, nobler general possibilities, greater gains, harder struggles; they say, "We are just as happy here." "It is easier to make a living in Kentucky than to keep from being run over in New York," said a young Kentuckian; and home he went.

If you attempt to deal with them in the business of the market-place, do not trick or cheat them. Above all things they hate and despise intrigue and deception. For one single act of dishonor a man will pay with life-long aversion and contempt. The rage it puts them in to be charged with lying themselves is the exact measure of the excitement with which they regard the lie in others. This is one of their idols—an idol of the market-place in the true

GENTLEMEN OF LEISURE

County Court Day in Kentucky

meaning of the Baconian philosophy. The new Kentuckian has not lost an old-time trait of character: so high and delicate a sense of personal honor that to be told he lies is the same as saying he has ceased to be a gentleman. Along with good faith and fair dealing goes liberality. Not prodigality; they have changed all that. The fresh system of things has produced no more decided result than a different regard for material interests. You shall not again charge the Kentuckians with lacking either "the telescopic appreciation of distant gain," or the microscopic appreciation of present gain. The influence of money is active, and the illusion of wealth become a reality. Profits are now more likely to pass into accumulation and structure. There is more discussion of costs and values. Small economies are more dwelt upon in thought and conversation. Actually you shall find the people higgling with the dealer over prices. And yet how significant a fact is it in their life that the merchant does not, as a rule, give exact change over the counter! At least the cent has not yet been put under the microscope.

Perhaps you will not accept it as an evidence of progress that so many men will leave their business all over the country for an idle day once a month in town—nay, oftener than once

County Court Day in Kentucky

a month ; for many who are at county court in this place to-day will attend it in another county next Monday. But do not be deceived by the lazy appearance of the streets. There are fewer idlers than of old. You may think this quiet group of men who have taken possession of a buggy or a curb-stone are out upon a costly holiday. Draw near, and it is discovered that there is fresh, eager, intelligent talk of the newest agricultural implements and of scientific farming. In fact, the day is to the assembled farmers the seed-time of ideas, to be scattered in ready soil—an informal, unconscious meeting of grangers.

There seems to be a striking equality of stations and conditions. Having travelled through many towns, and seen these gatherings together of all classes, you will be pleased with the fair, attractive, average prosperity, and note the almost entire absence of paupers and beggars. Somehow misfortune and ill-fortune and old age save themselves here from the last hard necessity of asking alms on the highway. But the appearance of the people will easily lead you to a wrong inference as to social equality. They are much less democratic than they seem, and their dress and speech and manners in the market-place are not their best equipment. You shall meet with these in their homes. In

County Court Day in Kentucky

their homes, too, social distinctions begin and are enforced, and men who find in the open square a common footing never associate elsewhere. But even among the best of the new Kentuckians will you hardly observe fidelity to the old social ideals, which adjudged that the very flower of birth and training must bloom in the bearing and deportment. With the crumbling and downfall of the old system fell also the structure of fine manners, which were at once its product and adornment.

VI

A NEW figure has made its appearance in the Kentucky market-place, having set its face resolutely towards the immemorial court-house and this periodic gathering together of freemen. Beyond comparison the most significant new figure that has made its way thither and cast its shadow on the people and the ground. Writ all over with problems that not the wisest can read. Stalking out of an awful past into what uncertain future! Clothed in hanging rags, it may be, or a garb that is a mosaic of strenuous patches. Ah! Pompey, or Cæsar, or Cicero, of the days of slavery, where be thy family carriage, thy master and mistress, now?

He comes into the county court, this old African, because he is a colored Kentuckian and must honor the stable customs of the country. He does little buying or selling; he is not a politician; he has no debt to collect, and no legal business. Still, example is powerful and

County Court Day in Kentucky

the negro imitative, so here he is at county court. It is one instance of the influence exerted over him by the institutions of the Kentuckian, so that he has a passion for fine stock, must build amphitheatres and hold fairs and attend races. Naturally, therefore, county court has become a great social day with his race. They stop work and come in from the country, or from the outskirts of the town, where they have congregated in little frame houses, and exhibit a quasi-activity in whatever of business and pleasure is going forward. In no other position of life does he exhibit his character and his condition more strikingly than here. Always comical, always tragical, light-hearted, sociable ; his shackles stricken off, but wearing those of his own indolence, ignorance, and helplessness ; the wandering Socrates of the streets, always dropping little shreds of observation on human affairs and bits of philosophy on human life; his memory working with last Sunday's sermon, and his hope with to-morrow's bread ; citizen, with so much freedom and so little liberty—the negro forms one of the conspicuous features of a county court day at the present time.

A wonderful, wonderful day this is that does thus always keep pace with civilization in the State, drawing all elements to itself, and por-

County Court Day in Kentucky

traying them to the interpreting eye. So that to paint the scenes of the county court days in the past is almost to write the history of the contemporary periods; and to do as much with one of the present hour is to depict the oldest influences that has survived and the newest that has been born in this local environment. To the future student of governmental and institutional history in this country, a study always interesting, always important, and always unique, will be county court day in Kentucky.

KENTUCKY FAIRS

I

THE nineteenth century opened gravely for the Kentuckians. Little akin as was the spirit of the people to that of the Puritans, life among them had been almost as granitic in its hardness and ruggedness and desolate unrelief. The only thing in the log-cabin that had sung from morning till night was the spinning-wheel. Not much behind those women but danger, anxiety, vigils, devastation, mournful tragedies; scarce one of them but might fitly have gone to her loom and woven herself a garment of sorrow. Not much behind those men but felling of trees, clearing of land, raising of houses, opening of roads, distressing problems of State, desolating wars of the republic. Most could remember the time when it was so common for a man to be killed, that to lie down and die a natural death seemed unnatural. Many must have had in their faces the sadness that was in the face of Lincoln.

Kentucky Fairs

Nevertheless, from the first, there had stood out among the Kentuckians broad exhibitions of exuberant animal vigor, of unbridled animal spirits. Some singularly and faithfully enough in the ancestral vein of English sports and relaxations—dog-fighting and cock-fighting, rifle target-shooting, wrestling matches, foot-racing for the men, and quarter-racing for the horses. Without any thought of making spectacles or of becoming themselves a spectacle in history, they were always ready to form an impromptu arena and institute athletic games. They had even their gladiators. Other rude pleasures were more characteristic of their environment —the log-rolling and the quilting, the social frolic of the harvesting, the merry parties of flax-pullers, and the corn-husking at nightfall, when the men divided into sides, and the green glass whiskey-bottle, stopped with a corn-cob, was filled and refilled and passed from mouth to mouth, until out of those lusty throats rose and swelled a rhythmic choral song that could be heard in the deep woods a mile or more away: at midnight those who were sober took home those who were drunk. But of course none of these were organized amusements. They are not instances of taking pleasures sadly, but of attempts to do much hard, rough work with gladness. Other occasions, also, which have

Kentucky Fairs

the semblance of popular joys, and which certainly were not passed over without merriment and turbulent, disorderly fun, were really set apart for the gravest of civic and political reasons: militia musters, stump-speakings, county court day assemblages, and the yearly July celebrations. Still other pleasures were of an economic or utilitarian nature. Thus the novel and exciting contests by parties of men at squirrel-shooting looked to the taking of that destructive animal's scalp, to say nothing of the skin; the hunting of beehives in the woods had some regard to the scarcity of sugar; and the nut gatherings and wild-grape gatherings by younger folks in the gorgeous autumnal days were partly in memory of a scant, unvaried larder, which might profitably draw upon nature's rich and salutary hoard. Perhaps the dearest pleasures among them were those that lay closest to their dangers. They loved the pursuit of marauding parties, the solitary chase; were always ready to throw away axe and mattock for rifle and knife. Among pleasures, certainly, should be mentioned the weddings. For plain reasons these were commonly held in the daytime. Men often rode to them armed, and before leaving too often made them scenes of carousal and unchastened jocularities. After the wedding came the "infare," with the going

Kentucky Fairs

from the home of the bride to the home of the groom. Above everything else that seems to strike the chord of common happiness in the society of the time, stands out to the imagination the picture of one of these processions—a long bridal cavalcade winding slowly along a narrow road through the silent, primeval forest, now in sunlight, now in the shadow of mighty trees meeting over the way; at the head the young lovers, so rudely mounted, so simply dressed, and, following in their happy wake, as though they were the augury of a peaceful era soon to come, a straggling, broken line of the men and women who had prepared for that era, but should never live to see its appearing.

Such scenes as these give a touch of bright, gay color to the dull homespun texture of the social fabric of the times. Indeed, when all the pleasures have been enumerated, they seem a good many. But the effect of such an enumeration is misleading. Life remained tense, sad, barren; character moulded itself on a model of Spartan simplicity and hardihood, without the Spartan treachery and cunning.

But from the opening of the nineteenth century things grew easier. The people, rescued from the necessity of trying to be safe, began to

Kentucky Fairs

indulge the luxury of wishing to be happy. Life ceased to be a warfare, and became an industry; the hand left off defending, and commenced acquiring; the moulding of bullets was succeeded by the coining of dollars.

II

IT is against the background of such a strenuous past that we find the Kentucky fair first projected by the practical and progressive spirit that ruled among the Kentuckians in the year 1816. Nothing could have been conceived with soberer purpose, or worn less the aspect of a great popular pleasure. Picture the scene! A distinguished soldier and honored gentleman, with a taste for agriculture and fine cattle, has announced that on a certain day in July he will hold on his farm a "Grand Cattle Show and Fair, free for everybody." The place is near Lexington, which was then the centre of commerce and seat of learning in the West. The meagre newspapers of the time have carried the tidings to every tavern and country cross-roads. It is a novel undertaking; the like has never been known this side of the Alleghanies. The summer morning come, you may see a very remarkable company of gentlemen: old pioneers, Revolu-

Kentucky Fairs

tionary soldiers, volunteers of the War of 1812, walking in picturesque twos and threes out of the little town to the green woods where the fair is to be held; others jogging thitherward along the by-paths and newly opened roads through the forest, clad in homespun from heel to head, and mindful of the cold lunches and whiskey-bottles in their coat-pockets or saddle-bags; some, perhaps, drawn thither in wagons and aristocratic gigs. Once arrived, all stepping around loftily on the velvet grass, peering curiously into each other's eyes, and offering their snuffboxes for a sneeze of convivial astonishment that they could venture to meet under the clear sky for such an undertaking. The five judges of the fair, coming from as many different counties, the greatest personages of their day—one, a brilliant judge of the Federal Court; the second, one of the earliest settlers, with a sword hanging up at home to show how Virginia appreciated his services in the Revolution: the third, a soldier and blameless gentleman of the old school; the fourth, one of the few early Kentuckians who brought into the new society the noble style of country-place, with park and deer, that would have done credit to an English lord; and the fifth, in no respect inferior to the others. These "perform the duties assigned them with assiduity," and hand

Kentucky Fairs

over to their neighbors as many as fifteen or twenty premium silver cups, costing twelve dollars apiece. After which the assemblage variously disperses—part through the woods again, while part return to town.

Such, then, was the first Kentucky fair. It was a transplantation to Kentucky, not of the English or European fair, but of the English cattle-show. It resembled the fair only in being a place for buying and selling. And it was not thought of in the light of a merry-making or great popular amusement. It seems not even to have taken account of manufactures—then so important an industry—or of agriculture.

Like the first was the second fair held in the same place the year following. Of this, little is and little need be known, save that then was formed the first State Agricultural Society of Kentucky, which also was the first in the West, and the second in the United States. This society held two or three annual meetings, and then went to pieces, but not before laying down the broad lines on which the fair continued to be held for the next quarter of a century. That is, the fair began as a cattle-show, though stock of other kinds was exhibited. Then it was extended to embrace agriculture; and with branches of good hus-

Kentucky Fairs

bandry it embraced as well those of good housewifery. Thus at the early fairs one finds the farmers contesting for premiums with their wheats and their whiskeys, while their skilful helpmates displayed the products—the never-surpassed products — of their looms: linens, cassinettes, jeans, and carpetings.

With this brief outline we may pass over the next twenty years. The current of State life during this interval ran turbulent and stormy. Now politics, now finance, imbittered and distressed the people. Time and again, here and there, small societies revived the fair, but all efforts to expand it were unavailing. And yet this period must be distinguished as the one during which the necessity of the fair became widely recognized; for it taught the Kentuckians that their chief interest lay in the soil, and that physical nature imposed upon them the agricultural type of life. Grass was to be their portion and their destiny. It taught them the insulation of their habitat, and the need of looking within their own society for the germs and laws of their development. As soon as the people came to see that they were to be a race of farmers, it is important to note their concern that, as such, they should be hedged with respectability. They took high ground about it; they would not cease to be

Kentucky Fairs

gentlemen; they would have their class well reputed for fat pastures and comfortable homes, but honored as well for manners and liberal intelligence. And to this end they had recourse to an agricultural literature. Thus, when the fair began to revive, with happier auspices, near the close of the period under consideration, they signalized it for nearly the quarter of a century afterwards by instituting literary contests. Prizes and medals were offered for discoveries and inventions which should be of interest to the Kentucky agriculturist; and hundreds of dollars were appropriated for the victors and the second victors in the writing of essays which should help the farmer to become a scientist and not to forget to remain a gentleman. In addition, they sometimes sat for hours in the open air while some eminent citizen—the Governor, if possible—delivered an address to commemorate the opening of the fair, and to review the progress of agricultural life in the commonwealth. But there were many anti-literarians among them, who conceived a sort of organized hostility to what they aspersed as book-farming, and on that account withheld their cordial support.

III

IT was not until about the year 1840 that the fair began to touch the heart of the whole people. Before this time there had been no amphitheatre, no music, no booths, no side-shows, no ladies. A fair without ladies! How could the people love it, or ever come to look upon it as their greatest annual occasion for love-making?

An interesting commentary on the social decorum of this period is furnished in the fact that for some twenty years after the institution of the fair no woman put her foot upon the ground. She was thought a bold woman, doing a bold deed, who one day took a friend and, under the escort of gentlemen, drove in her own carriage to witness the showing of her own fat cattle; for she was herself one of the most practical and successful of Kentucky farmers. But where one of the sex has been, may not all the sex — may not all the world —safely follow? From the date of this event,

Kentucky Fairs

and the appearance of women on the grounds, the tide of popular favor set in steadily towards the fair.

For, as an immediate consequence, seats must be provided. Here one happens upon a curious bit of local history—the evolution of the amphitheatre among the Kentuckians. At the earliest fairs the first form of the amphitheatre had been a rope stretched from tree to tree, while the spectators stood around on the outside, or sat on the grass or in their vehicles. The immediate result of the necessity for providing comfortable seats for the now increasing crowd, was to select as a place for holding the fair such a site as the ancient Greeks might have chosen for building a theatre. Sometimes this was the head of a deep ravine, around the sides of which seats were constructed, while the bottom below served as the arena for the exhibition of the stock, which was led in and out through the mouth of the hollow. At other times advantage was taken of a natural sink and semicircular hill-side. The slope was sodded and terraced with rows of seats, and the spectators looked down upon the circular basin at the bottom. But clearly enough the sun played havoc with the complexions of the ladies, and a sudden drenching shower was still one of the uncomfortable dispensations of Prov-

Kentucky Fairs

idence. Therefore a roofed wooden structure of temporary seats made its appearance, designed after the fashion of those used by the travelling show, and finally out of this form came the closed circular amphitheatre, modelled on the plan of the Colosseum. Thus first among the Kentuckians, if I mistake not, one saw the English cattle-show, which meantime was gathering about itself many characteristics of the English fair, wedded strangely enough to the temple of a Roman holiday. By-and-by we shall see this form of amphitheatre torn down and supplanted by another, which recalls the ancient circle or race-course—a modification corresponding with a change in the character of the later fair.

The most desirable spot for building the old circular amphitheatre was some beautiful tract of level ground containing from five to twenty acres, and situated near a flourishing town and its ramifying turnpikes. This track must be enclosed by a high wooden paling, with here and there entrance gates for stock and pedestrians and vehicles, guarded by gate-keepers. And within this enclosure appeared in quick succession all the varied accessories that went to make up a typical Kentucky fair near the close of the old social regime; that is, before the outbreak of the Civil War.

Kentucky Fairs

Here were found the hundreds of neat stalls for the different kinds of stock; the gay booths under the colonnade of the amphitheatre for refreshments; the spacious cottages for women and invalids and children; the platforms of the quack-doctors; the floral hall and the pagoda-like structure for the musicians and the judges; the tables and seats for private dining; the high swings and the turnabouts; the tests of the strength of limb and lung; the gaudy awnings for the lemonade venders; the huge brown hogsheads for iced-water, with bright tin cups dangling from the rim; the circus; and, finally, all those tented spectacles of the marvellous, the mysterious, and the monstrous which were to draw popular attention to the Kentucky fair, as they had been the particular delight of the fair-going thousands in England hundreds of years before.

For you will remember that the Kentucky fair has ceased by this time to be a cattle-show. It has ceased to be simply a place for the annual competitive exhibition of stock of all kinds, which, by-the-way, is beginning to make the country famous. It has ceased to be even the harvest-home of the Blue-grass Region, the mild autumnal saturnalia of its rural population. Whatever the people can discover or invent is indeed here; or whatever they

Kentucky Fairs

own, or can produce from the bountiful earth, or take from orchard or flower-garden, or make in dairy, kitchen, or loom-room. But the fair is more than all this now. It has become the great yearly pleasure-ground of the people assembled for a week's festivities. It is what the European fair of old was—the season of the happiest and most general intercourse between country and town. Here the characteristic virtues and vices of the local civilization will be found in open flower side by side, and types and manners painted to the eye in vividest colorings.

Crowded picture of a time gone by! Bright glancing pageantry of life, moving on with feasting and music and love-making to the very edge of the awful precipice, over which its social system and its richly nurtured ideals will be dashed to pieces below!—why not pause an instant over its innocent mirth and quick, awful tragedies?

IV

THE fair has been in progress several days, and this will be the greatest day of all: nothing shown from morning till night but horses—horses in harness, horses under the saddle. Ah! but *that* will be worth seeing! Late in the afternoon the little boys will ride for premiums on their ponies, and, what is not so pretty, but far more exciting, young men will contest the prize of horsemanship. And then such racking and pacing and loping and walking!—such racing round and round and round to see who can go fastest, and be gracefulest, and turn quickest! Such pirouetting and curveting and prancing and cavorting and riding with arms folded across the breast while the reins lie on the horse's neck, and suddenly bowing over to the horse's mane, as some queen of beauty high up in the amphitheatre, transported by the excitement of the thousands of spectators and the closeness of the contest, throws her flowers and handkerchief down

HARNESS HORSES

Kentucky Fairs

into the arena! Ah, yes! this will be the great day at the fair—at the modern tourney!

So the tide of the people is at the flood. For days they have been pouring into the town. The hotels are overflowing with strangers; the open houses of the citizens are full of guests. Strolling companies of players will crack the dusty boards to-night with the tread of buskin and cothurnus. The easy-going tradespeople have trimmed their shops, and imported from the North their richest merchandise.

From an early hour of the morning, along every road that leads from country or town to the amphitheatre, pour the hurrying throng of people, eager to get good seats for the day; for there will be thousands not seated at all. Streaming out, on the side of the town, are pedestrians, hacks, omnibuses, the negro drivers shouting, racing, cracking their whips, and sometimes running into the way-side stands where old negro women are selling apples and gingerbread. Streaming in, on the side of the country, are pedestrians, heated, their coats thrown over the shoulder or the arm; buggies containing often a pair of lovers who do not keep their secret discreetly; family carriages with children made conspicuously tidy and mothers aglow with the recent labors of the kitchen: comfortable evidences of which are

Kentucky Fairs

the huge baskets or hampers that are piled up in front or strapped on behind. Nay, sometimes may be seen whole wagon-loads of provisions moving slowly in, guarded by portly negresses, whose eyes shine like black diamonds through the setting of their white-dusted eyelashes.

Within the grounds, how rapidly the crowd swells and surges hither and thither, tasting the pleasures of the place before going to the amphitheatre: to the stalls, to the booths, to the swings, to the cottage, to the floral hall, to the living curiosities, to the swinish pundits, who have learned their lessons in numbers and cards. Is not that the same pig that was shown at Bartholomew's four centuries ago? Mixed in with the Kentuckians are people of a different build and complexion. For Kentucky now is one of the great summering States for the extreme Southerners, who come up with their families to its watering-places. Others who are scattered over the North return in the autumn by way of Kentucky, remaining till the fair and the fall of the first frost. Nay, is not the State the place for the reunion of families that have Southern members? Back to the old home from the rice and sugar and cotton plantations of the swamps and the bayous come young Kentucky wives with Southern

Kentucky Fairs

husbands, young Kentucky husbands with Southern wives. All these are at the fair—the Lexington fair. Here, too, are strangers from wellnigh every Northern State. And, I beg you, do not overlook the negroes—a solid acre of them. They play unconsciously a great part in the essential history of this scene and festival. Briskly grooming the stock in the stalls; strolling around with carriage whips in their hands; running on distant errands; showering a tumult of blows upon the newly arrived "boss" with their nimble, ubiquitous brush-brooms; everywhere, everywhere, happy, well-dressed, sleek—the fateful background of all this stage of social history.

But the amphitheatre! Through the mild, chastened, soft-toned atmosphere of the early September day the sunlight falls from the unclouded sky upon the seated thousands. Ah, the women in all their silken and satin bravery! delicate blue and pink and canary-colored petticoats, with muslin over-dresses, black lace and white lace mantles, white kid gloves, and boots to match the color of their petticoats. One stands up to allow a lemonade-seller to pass; she wears a hoop-skirt twelve feet in circumference. Here and there costumes suitable for a ball; arms and shoulders glistening like marble in the sunlight; gold chains

Kentucky Fairs

around the delicate arching necks. Oh, the jewels, the flowers, the fans, the parasols, the ribbons, the soft eyes and smiles, the love and happiness! And some of the complexions!—paint on the cheeks, powder on the neck, stick-pomatum plastering the beautiful hair down over the temples. No matter; it is the fashion. Rub it in! Rub it in well—up to the very roots of the hair and eyebrows! Now, how perfect you are, madam! You are the great Kentucky show of life-size wax-works.

In another part of the amphitheatre nothing but men, red-faced, excited, standing up on the seats, shouting, applauding, as the rival horses rush round the ring before them. It is not difficult to know who these are. The money streams through their fingers. Did you hear the crack of that pistol? How the crowd swarms angrily. Stand back! A man has been shot. He insulted a gentleman. He called him a liar. Be careful. There are a great many pistols on the fair grounds.

In all the United States where else is there to be seen any such holiday assemblage of people—any such expression of the national life impressed with local peculiarities? Where else is there to be seen anything that, while it falls far behind, approaches so near the spirit of uproarious merriment, of reckless fun, which

Kentucky Fairs

used to intoxicate and madden the English populace when given over to the sports of a ruder age? These are the descendants of the sad pioneers — of those early cavalcades which we glanced at in the primeval forests a few minutes ago. These have subdued the land, and are reclining on its tranquil autumn fulness. Time enough to play now — more time than there ever was before; more than there will ever be again. They have established their great fair here on the very spot where their forefathers were massacred or put to torture. So, at old Smithfield, the tumblers, the jesters, the buffoons, and the dancers shouldered each other in joyful riot over the ashes of the earlier heroes and martyrs.

It is past high noon, and the thousands break away from the amphitheatre and move towards a soft green woodland in another part of the grounds, shaded by forest trees. Here are the private dinner-tables — hundreds of them, covered with snowy linen, glittering with glass and silver. You have heard of Kentucky hospitality; here you will see one of the peaceful battle-fields where reputation for that virtue is fought for and won. Is there a stranger among these thousands that has not been hunted up and provided for? And

Kentucky Fairs

such dinners! Old Pepys should be here—immortal eater—so that he could go home and set down in his diary, along with other gastronomic adventures, garrulous notes of what he saw eaten and ate himself at the Kentucky fair. You will never see the Kentuckians making a better show than at this moment. What courtesy, what good-will, what warm and gracious manners! Tie a blue ribbon on them. In a competitive exhibition of this kind the premium will stay at home.

But make the most of it—make the most of this harmony. For did you see that? A father and a son met each other, turned their heads quickly and angrily away, and passed without speaking.

Look how these two men shake hands with too much cordiality, and search each other's eyes. There is a man from the North standing apart and watching with astonishment these alert, happy, efficient negroes—perhaps following with his thoughtful gaze one of Mrs. Stowe's Uncle Toms. A Southerner has drawn that Kentucky farmer beside a tree, and is trying to buy one of these servants for his plantation. Yes, yes, make the most of it! The war is coming. It is in men's hearts, and in their eyes and consciences. By-and-by this bright, gay pageant will pass so entirely away

Kentucky Fairs

that even the thought of it will come back to one like the unsubstantial revelry of a dream. By-and-by there will be another throng filling these grounds: not in pink and white and canary, but in blue, solid blue—blue overcoats, showing sad and cold above the snow. All round the amphitheatre tents will be spread— not covering, as now, the hideous and the monstrous, but the sleeping forms of young men, athletic, sinewy, beautiful. This, too, shall vanish. And some day, when the fierce summer sun is killing the little gray leaves and blades of grass, in through these deserted gates will pass a long, weary, foot-sore line of brown. Nothing in the floral hall now but cots, around which are nurses and weeping women. Lying there, some poor young fellow, with the death dew on his forehead, will open his shadowy eyes and remember this day of the fair, where he walked among the flowers and made love.

But it is late in the afternoon, and the people are beginning to disperse by turnpike and lane to their homes in the country, or to hasten back into town for the festivities of the night; for to-night the spirit of the fair will be continued in other amphitheatres. To-night comedy and tragedy will tread the village boards; but hand in hand also they will

Kentucky Fairs

flaunt their colors through the streets, and haunt the midnight alleys. In all the year no time like fair-time: parties at private houses; hops, balls at the hotels. You shall sip the foam from the very crest of the wave of revelry and carousal. Darkness be over it till the east reddens! Let Bacchus be unconfined!

V

THE fair languished during the war, but the people were not slow to revive it upon the return of peace. Peace, however, could never bring back the fair of the past: it was gone forever—gone with the stage and phase of the social evolution of which it was the unique and memorable expression. For there was no phase of social evolution in Kentucky but felt profoundly that era of upheaval, drift, and readjustment. Start where we will, or end where we may, we shall always come sooner or later to the war as a great rent and chasm, with its hither side and its farther side and its deep abyss between, down into which old things were dashed to death, and out of which new things were born into the better life.

Therefore, as we study the Kentucky fair of to-day, more than a quarter of a century later, we must expect to find it much changed. Withal it has many local variations. As it is

Kentucky Fairs

held here and there in retired counties or by little neighborhoods it has characteristics of rural picturesqueness that suggest the manners of the era passed away. But the typical Kentucky fair, the fair that represents the leading interests and advanced ideas of the day, bears testimony enough to the altered life of the people.

The old circular amphitheatre has been torn down, and replaced with a straight or a slightly curved bank of seats. Thus we see the arena turned into the race-course, the idea of the Colosseum giving way to the idea of the Circus Maximus. In front of the bank of seats stretch a small track for the exhibition of different kinds of stock, and a large track for the races. This abandonment of the old form of amphitheatre is thus a significant concession to the trotting-horse, and a sign that its speed has become the great pleasure of the fair.

As a picture, also, the fair of to-day lacks the Tyrolean brightness of its predecessors; and as a social event it seems like a pensive tale of by-gone merriment. Society no longer looks upon it as the occasion of displaying its wealth, its toilets, its courtesies, its hospitalities. No such gay and splendid dresses now; no such hundreds of dinner-tables on the shaded greensward. It would be too much to

Kentucky Fairs

say that the disappearance of the latter betokens the loss of that virtue which the gracious usages of a former time made a byword. The explanation lies elsewhere. Under the old social regime a common appurtenance to every well-established household was a trained force of negro servants. It was the services of these that made the exercise of generous public entertainment possible to the Kentucky housewife. Moreover, the lavish ideals of the time threw upon economy the reproach of meanness; and, as has been noted, the fair was then the universally recognized time for the display of munificent competitive hospitalities. In truth, it was the sharpness of the competition that brought in at last the general disuse of the custom; for the dinners grew more and more sumptuous, the labor of preparing them more and more severe, and the expense of paying for them more and more burdensome. So today the Kentuckians remain a hospitable people, but you must not look to find the noblest exercise of their hospitality at the fair. A few dinners you will see, but modest luncheons are not despicable, and the whole tendency of things is towards the understanding that an appetite is an affair of the private conscience. And this brings to light some striking differences between the old and the new Kentuck-

Kentucky Fairs

ians. Along with the circular amphitheatre, the dresses, and the dinners, have gone the miscellaneous amusements of which the fair was erewhile the mongrel scene and centre. The ideal fair of to-day frowns upon the side-show, and discards every floating accessory. It would be self-sufficient. It would say to the thousands of people who still attend it as the greatest of all their organized pleasures, " Find your excitement, your relaxation, your happiness, in a shed for machinery, a floral hall, and the fine stock." But of these the greatest attraction is the last, and of all kinds of stock the one most honored is the horse. Here, then, we come upon a noteworthy fact : the Kentucky fair, which began as a cattle-show, seems likely to end with being a horse-show.

If anything is lacking to complete the contrast between the fair in the fulness of its development before the war and the fair of to-day, what better could be found to reflect this than the different *morale* of the crowd?

You are a stranger, and you have the impression that an assemblage of ten, fifteen, twenty thousand Kentuckians out on a holiday is pervaded by the spirit of a mob. You think that a few broken heads is one of its cherished traditions; that intoxication and disorderliness are its dearest prerogatives. But

Kentucky Fairs

nowadays you look in vain for those heated, excited men with money lying between their fingers, who were once the rebuke and the terror of the amphitheatre. You look in vain for heated, excited men of any kind : there are none. There is no drinking, no bullying, no elbowing, or shouldering, or swearing.

While still in their nurses' arms you may sometimes see the young Kentuckians shown in the ring at the horse-fair for premiums. From their early years they are taken to the amphitheatre to enjoy its color, its fleetness, and its form. As little boys they ride for prizes. The horse is the subject of talk in the hotels, on the street corners, in the saloons, at the stables, on county court day, at the cross-roads and blacksmiths' shops, in country church-yards before the sermon. The barber, as he shaves his morning customer, gives him points on the races. There will be found many a group of gentlemen in whose presence to reveal an ignorance of famous horses and common pedigrees will bring a blush to the cheek. Not to feel interested in such themes is to lay one's self open to a charge of disagreeable eccentricity. The horse has gradually emerged into prominence until to-day it occupies the foreground.

A HOME OF THE SILENT BROTHERHOOD

I

MORE than two hundred and fifty years have passed since the Cardinal de Richelieu stood at the baptismal font as sponsor to a name that within the pale of the Church was destined to become more famous than his own. But the world has wellnigh forgotten Richelieu's godson. Only the tireless student of biography now turns the pages that record his extraordinary career, ponders the strange unfolding of his moral nature, is moved by the deep pathos of his dying hours. Dominique Armand-Jean Le Bouthillier de Rancé! How cleverly, while scarcely out of short-clothes, did he puzzle the king's confessor with questions on Homer, and at the age of thirteen publish an edition of Anacreon! Of ancient, illustrious birth, and heir to an almost ducal house, how tenderly favored was he by Marie de Médicis; happy-hearted, kindly, suasive, how idolized by a gorgeous court! In what affluence of

A Home of the Silent Brotherhood

rich laces did he dress; in what irresistible violet-colored close coats, with emeralds at his wristbands, a diamond on his finger, red heels on his shoes! How nimbly he capered through the dance with a sword on his hip! How bravely he planned quests after the manner of knights of the Round Table, meaning to take for himself the part of Lancelot! How exquisitely, ardently, and ah! how fatally he flirted with the incomparable ladies in the circle of Madame de Rambouillet! And with a zest for sport as great as his unction for the priestly office, how wittily — laying one hand on his heart and waving the other through the air—could he bow and say, "This morning I preached like an angel; I'll hunt like the devil this afternoon!"

All at once his life broke in two when half spent. He ceased to hunt like the devil, to adore the flesh, to scandalize the world; and retiring to the ancient Abbey of La Trappe in Normandy — the sponsorial gift of his Eminence and favored by many popes—there undertook the difficult task of reforming the relaxed Benedictines. The old abbey—situated in a great fog-covered basin encompassed by dense woods of beech, oak, and linden, and therefore gloomy, unhealthy, and forbidding —was in ruins. One ascended by means of a

A Home of the Silent Brotherhood

ladder from floor to rotting floor. The refectory had become a place where the monks assembled to play at bowls with worldlings. The dormitory, exposed to wind, rain, and snow, had been given up to owls. In the church the stones were scattered, the walls unsteady, the pavement was broken, the bell ready to fall. As a single solemn reminder of the vanished spirit of the place, which had been founded by St. Stephen and St. Bernard in the twelfth century, with the intention of reviving in the Western Church the bright examples of primitive sanctity furnished by Eastern solitaries of the third and fourth, one read over the door of the cloister the words of Jeremiah: "*Sedebit solitarius et tacebit.*" The few monks who remained in the convent slept where they could, and were, as Chateaubriand says, in a state of ruins. They preferred sipping ratafia to reading their breviaries; and when De Rancé undertook to enforce reform, they threatened to whip him for his pains. He, in turn, threatened them with the royal interference, and they submitted. There, accordingly, he introduced a system of rules that a sybarite might have wept over even to hear recited; carried into practice cenobitical austerities that recalled the models of pious anchorites in Syria and Thebais; and gave its

A Home of the Silent Brotherhood

peculiar meaning to the word "Trappist," a name which has since been taken by all Cistercian communities embracing the reform of the first monastery.

In the retirement of this mass of woods and sky De Rancé passed the rest of his long life, doing nothing more worldly, so far as is now known, than quoting Aristophanes and Horace to Bossuet, and allowing himself to be entertained by Pellisson, exhibiting the accomplishments of his educated spider. There, in acute agony of body and perfect meekness of spirit, a worn and weary old man, with time enough to remember his youthful ardors and emeralds and illusions, he watched his mortal end draw slowly near. And there, asking to be buried in some desolate spot—some old battle-field—he died at last, extending his poor macerated body on the cross of blessed cinders and straw, and commending his poor penitent soul to the mercy of Heaven.

A wonderful spectacle to the less fervid Benedictines of the closing seventeenth century must have seemed the work of De Rancé in that old Norman abbey! A strange company of human souls, attracted by the former distinction of the great abbot as well as by the peculiar vows of the institute, must have come together in its silent halls! One hears many

A Home of the Silent Brotherhood

stories, in the lighter vein, regarding some of its inmates. Thus, there was a certain furious ex-trooper, lately reeking with blood, who got himself much commended by living on baked apples; and a young nobleman who devoted himself to the work of washing daily the monastery spittoons. One Brother, the story runs, having one day said there was too much salt in his scalding-hot broth, immediately burst into tears of contrition for his wickedness in complaining; and another went for so many years without raising his eyes that he knew not a new chapel had been built, and so quite cracked his skull one day against the wall of it.

The abbey was an asylum for the poor and helpless, the shipwrecked, the conscience-stricken, and the broken-hearted — for that meditative type of fervid piety which for ages has looked upon the cloister as the true earthly paradise wherein to rear the difficult edifice of the soul's salvation. Much noble blood sought De Rancé's retreat to wash out its terrifying stains, and more than one reckless spirit went thither to take upon itself the yoke of purer, sweeter usages.

De Rancé's work remains an influence in the world. His monastery and his reform constitute the true background of material and

A Home of the Silent Brotherhood

spiritual fact against which to outline the present Abbey of La Trappe in Kentucky. Even when thus viewed, it seems placed where it is only by some freak of history. An abbey of La Trappe in Kentucky! How inharmonious with every element of its environment appears this fragment of old French monastic life! It is the twelfth century touching the last of the nineteenth—the Old World reappearing in the New. Here are French faces — here is the French tongue. Here is the identical white cowl presented to blessed St. Alberick in the forests of Burgundy nine hundred years ago. Here is the rule of St. Benedict, patriarch of the Western monks in the sixth century. When one is put out at the way-side station, amid woodlands and fields of Indian-corn, and, leaving the world behind him, turns his footsteps across the country towards the abbey, more than a mile away, the seclusion of the region, its ineffable quietude, the infinite isolation of the life passed by the silent brotherhood—all bring vividly before the mind the image of that ancient distant abbey with which this one holds connection so sacred and so close. Is it not the veritable spot in Normandy? Here, too, is the broad basin of retired country; here the densely wooded hills, shutting it in from the world; here the orchards

A Home of the Silent Brotherhood

and vineyards and gardens of the ascetic devotees; and, as the night falls from the low, blurred sky of gray, and cuts short a silent contemplation of the scene, here, too, one finds one's self, like some belated traveller in the dangerous forests of old, hurrying on to reach the porter's lodge, and ask within the sacred walls the hospitality of the venerable abbot.

FOR nearly a century after the death of De Rancé it is known that his followers faithfully maintained his reform at La Trappe. Then the French Revolution drove the Trappists as wanderers into various countries, and the abbey was made a foundery for cannon. A small branch of the order came in 1804 to the United States, and established itself for a while in Pennsylvania, but soon turned its eyes towards the greater wilds and solitudes of Kentucky. For this there was reason. Kentucky was early a great pioneer of the Catholic Church in the United States. Here the first episcopal see of the West was erected, and Bardstown held spiritual jurisdiction, within certain parallels of latitude, over all States and Territories between the two oceans. Here, too, were the first Catholic missionaries of the West, except those who were to be found in the French stations along the Wabash and the Mississippi. Indeed, the Cath-

A Home of the Silent Brotherhood

olic population of Kentucky, which was principally descended from the colonists of Lord Baltimore, had begun to enter the State as early as 1775, the nucleus of their settlements soon becoming Nelson County, the locality of the present abbey. Likewise it should be remembered that the Catholic Church in the United States, especially that portion of it in Kentucky, owes a great debt to the zeal of the exiled French clergy of early days. That buoyancy and elasticity of the French character, which naturally adapts it to every circumstance and emergency, was then most demanded and most efficacious. From these exiles the infant missions of the State were supplied with their most devoted laborers.

Hither, accordingly, the Trappists removed from Pennsylvania, establishing themselves on Pottinger's Creek, near Rohan's Knob, several miles from the present site. But they remained only a few years. The climate of Kentucky was ill-suited to their life of unrelaxed asceticism; their restless superior had conceived a desire to christianize Indian children, and so removed the languishing settlement to Missouri. There is not space for following the solemn march of those austere exiles through the wildernesses of the New World. From Missouri they went to an ancient Indian burying-ground in Illinois,

A Home of the Silent Brotherhood

and there built up a sort of village in the heart of the prairie; but the great mortality from which they suffered, and the subsidence of the fury of the French Revolution recalled them in 1813 to France, to reoccupy the establishments from which they had been banished.

It was of this body that Dickens, in his *American Notes*, wrote as follows:

Looming up in the distance, as we rode along, was another of the ancient Indian burial-places, called Monk's Mound, in memory of a body of fanatics of the order of La Trappe, who founded a desolate convent there many years ago, when there were no settlements within a thousand miles, and were all swept off by the pernicious climate; in which lamentable fatality few rational people will suppose, perhaps, that society experienced any very severe deprivation.

This is a better place in which to state a miracle than discuss it; and the following account of a heavenly portent, which is related to have been vouchsafed the Trappists while sojourning in Kentucky, may be given without comment:

In the year 1808 the moon, being then about two-thirds full, presented a most remarkable appearance. A bright, luminous cross, clearly defined, was seen in the heavens, with its arms intersecting the centre of the moon. On each side two smaller crosses were also distinctly visible, though the portions of them

A Home of the Silent Brotherhood

most distant from the moon were more faintly marked. This strange phenomenon continued for several hours, and was witnessed by the Trappists on their arising, as usual, at midnight, to sing the Divine praise.

The present monastery, which is called the Abbey of Gethsemane, owes its origin immediately to the Abbey of La Meilleraye, of the department of the Loire-Inférieure, France. The abbot of the latter had concluded arrangements with the French Government to found a house in the island of Martinique, on an estate granted by Louis Philippe; but this monarch's rule having been overturned, the plan was abandoned in favor of a colony in the United States. Two Fathers, with the view of selecting a site, came to New York in the summer of 1848, and naturally turned their eyes to the Catholic settlements in Kentucky, and to the domain of the pioneer Trappists. In the autumn of that year, accordingly, about forty-five "religious" left the mother-abbey of La Meilleraye, set sail from Havre de Grace for New Orleans, went thence by boat to Louisville, and from this point walked to Gethsemane, a distance of some sixty miles. Although scattered among various countries of Europe, the Trappists have but two convents in the United States—this, the oldest, and one near Dubuque, Iowa, a colony from the abbey in Ireland.

III

THE domain of the abbey comprises some seventeen hundred acres of land, part of which is tillable, while the rest consists of a range of wooded knobs that furnish timber to the monastery steam saw-mill. Around this domain lie the homesteads of Kentucky farmers, who make indifferent monks. One leaves the public road that winds across the open country and approaches the monastery through a long, level avenue, enclosed on each side by a hedge-row of cedars, and shaded by nearly a hundred beautiful English elms, the offspring of a single parent stem. Traversing this dim, sweet spot, where no sound is heard but the waving of boughs and the softened notes of birds, one reaches the porter's lodge, a low, brick building, on each side of which extends the high brick-wall that separates the inner from the outer world. Passing beneath the archway of the lodge, one discovers a graceful bit of landscape gardening—walks fringed with

A Home of the Silent Brotherhood

cedars, beds for flowers, pathways so thickly strewn with sawdust that the heaviest footfall is unheard, a soft turf of green, disturbed only by the gentle shadows of the pious-looking Benedictine trees; a fit spot for recreation and meditation. It is with a sort of worldly start that you come upon an enclosure at one end of these grounds wherein a populous family of white-cowled rabbits trip around in the most noiseless fashion, and seemed ashamed of being caught living together in family relations.

Architecturally there is little to please the æsthetic sense in the monastery building, along the whole front of which these grounds extend. It is a great quadrangular pile of brick, three stories high, heated by furnaces and lighted by gas—modern appliances which heighten the contrast with the ancient life whose needs they subserve. Within the quadrangle is a green inner court, also beautifully laid off. On one side are two chapels, the one appropriated to the ordinary services of the Church, and entered from without the abbey-wall by all who desire; the other, consecrated to the offices of the Trappist order, entered only from within, and accessible exclusively to males. It is here that one finds occasion to remember the Trappist's vow of poverty. The vestments are far from rich, the decorations of the altar far from

A Home of the Silent Brotherhood

splendid. The crucifixion-scene behind the altar consists of wooden figures carved by one of the monks now dead, and painted with little art. No tender light of many hues here streams through long windows rich with holy reminiscence and artistic fancy. The church has, albeit, a certain beauty of its own—that charm which is inseparable from fine proportion in stone and from gracefully disposed columns growing into the arches of the lofty roof. But the cold gray of the interior, severe and unrelieved, bespeaks a place where the soul comes to lay itself in simplicity before the Eternal as it would upon a naked, solitary rock of the desert. Elsewhere in the abbey greater evidences of votive poverty occur—in the various statues and shrines of the Virgin, in the pictures and prints that hang in the main front corridor—in all that appertains to the material life of the community.

Just outside the church, beneath the perpetual benediction of the cross on its spire, is the quiet cemetery garth, where the dead are side by side, their graves covered with myrtle and having each for its headstone a plain wooden crucifix bearing the religious name and station of him who lies below—Father Honorius, Father Timotheus, Brother Hilarius, Brother Eutropius. Who are they? And

A Home of the Silent Brotherhood

whence? And by what familiar names were they greeted on the old play-grounds and battle-fields of the world?

The Trappists do not, as it is commonly understood, daily dig a portion of their own graves. When one of them dies and has been buried, a new grave is begun beside the one just filled, as a reminder to the survivors that one of them must surely take his place therein. So, too, when each seeks the cemetery enclosure, in hours of holy meditation, and, standing bareheaded among the graves, prays softly for the souls of his departed brethren, he may come for a time to this unfinished grave, and, kneeling, pray Heaven, if he be next, to dismiss his soul in peace.

Nor do they sleep in the dark, abject kennel, which the imagination, in the light of mediæval history, constructs as the true monk's cell. By the rule of St. Benedict, they sleep separate, but in the same dormitory—a great upper room, well lighted and clean, in the body of which a general framework several feet high is divided into partitions that look like narrow berths.

IV

WE have acquired poetical and pictorial conceptions of monks—praying with wan faces and upturnęd eyes half darkened by the shadowing cowl, the coarse serge falling away from the emaciated neck, the hands pressing the crucifix close to the heart; and with this type has been associated a certain idea of cloistral life—that it was an existence of vacancy and idleness, or at best of deep meditation of the soul broken only by express spiritual devotions. There is another kind of monk, with the marks of which we seem traditionally familiar: the monk with the rubicund face, sleek poll, good epigastric development, and slightly unsteady gait, with whom, in turn, we have connected a different phase of conventual discipline—fat capon and stubble goose, and midnight convivial chantings growing ever more fast and furious, but finally dying away in a heavy stertorous calm. Poetry, art, the drama, the novel, have each portrayed

A Home of the Silent Brotherhood

human nature in orders; the saint-like monk, the intellectual monk, the bibulous, the felonious, the fighting monk (who loves not the hermit of Copmanhurst?), until the memory is stored and the imagination preoccupied.

Living for a while in a Trappist monastery in modern America, one gets a pleasant actual experience of other types no less picturesque and on the whole much more acceptable. He finds himself, for one thing, brought face to face with the working monk. Idleness to the Trappist is the enemy of the soul, and one of his vows is manual labor. Whatever a monk's previous station may have been, he must perform, according to abbatial direction, the most menial services. None are exempt from work; there is no place among them for the sluggard. When it is borne in mind that the abbey is a self-dependent institution, where the healthy must be maintained, the sick cared for, the dead buried, the necessity for much work becomes manifest. In fact, the occupations are as various as those of a modern factory. There is scope for intellects of all degrees and talents of wellnigh every order. Daily life, unremittingly from year to year, is an exact system of duties and hours. The building, covering about an acre of ground and penetrated by corridors, must be kept faultlessly clean. There

A Home of the Silent Brotherhood

are three kitchens—one for the guests, one for the community, and one for the infirmary—that require each a *coquinarius* and separate assistants. There is a tinker's shop and a pharmacy; a saddlery, where the broken gear used in cultivating the monastery lands is mended; a tailor's shop, where the worn garments are patched; a shoemaker's shop, where the coarse, heavy shoes of the monks are made and cobbled; and a barber's shop, where the Trappist beard is shaved twice a month and the Trappist head is monthly shorn.

Out-doors the occupations are even more varied. The community do not till the farm. The greater part of their land is occupied by tenant farmers, and what they reserve for their own use is cultivated by the so-called "family brothers," who, it is due to say, have no families, but live as celibates on the abbey domain, subject to the abbot's authority, without being members of the order. The monks, however, do labor in the ample gardens, orchards, and vineyard, from which they derive their sustenance, in the steam saw-mill and grain-mill, in the dairy and the cheese factory. Thus picturesquely engaged one may find them in autumn: monks gathering apples and making pungent cider, which is stored away in the vast cellar as their only beverage except water;

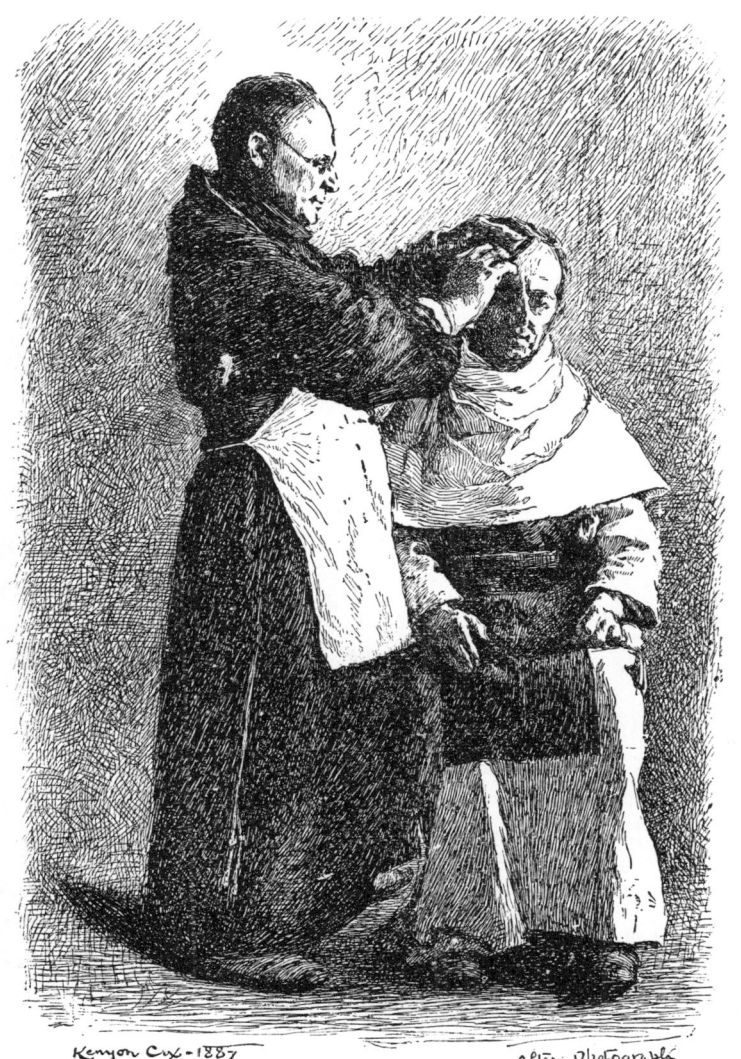

A FORTNIGHTLY SHAVE

A Home of the Silent Brotherhood

monks repairing the shingle roof of a stable; monks feeding the huge swine, which they fatten for the board of their carnal guests, or the fluttering multitude of chickens, from the eggs and young of which they derive a slender revenue; monks grouped in the garden around a green and purple heap of turnips, to be stored up as a winter relish of no mean distinction. Amid such scenes one forgets all else while enjoying the wealth and freshness of artistic effects. What a picture is this young Belgian cheese-maker, his sleeves rolled above the elbows of his brawny arms, his great pinkish hands buried in the golden curds, the cap of his serge cloak falling back and showing his closely clipped golden-brown hair, blue eyes, and clear, delicate skin! Or this Australian ex-farmer, as he stands by the hopper of grist or lays on his shoulder a bag of flour for the coarse brown-bread of the monks. Or this dark old French opera singer, who strutted his brief hour on many a European stage, but now hobbles around, hoary in his cowl and blanched with age, to pick up a handful of garlic. Or this athletic young Irishman, thrusting a great iron prod into the glowing coals of the sawmill furnace. Or this slender Switzer, your attendant in the refectory, with great keys dangling from his leathern cincture, who stands by

A Home of the Silent Brotherhood

with folded hands and bowed head while you are eating the pagan meal he has prepared for you.

From various countries of the Old World men find their way into the Abbey of Gethsemane, but among them are no Americans. Repeatedly the latter have joined the order, and have failed to persevere up to the final consecration of the white cowl. The fairest warning is given to the postulant. He is made to understand the entire extent of the obligation he has assumed; and only after passing through a novitiate, prolonged at the discretion of the abbot, is he admitted to the vows that must be kept unbroken till death.

V

FROM the striking material aspects of their daily life, one is soon recalled to a sense of their subordination to spiritual aims and pledges; for upon them, like a spell of enchantment, lies the sacred silence. The honey has been taken from the bees with solemnity; the grapes have been gathered without song and mirth. The vow of life-long silence taken by the Trappist must of course not be construed literally; but there are only two occasions during which it is completely set aside —when confessing his sins and when singing the offices of the Church. At all other times his tongue becomes, as far as possible, a superfluous member; he speaks only by permission of his superior, and always simply and to the point. The monk at work with another exchanges with him only the few low, necessary words, and those that provoke no laughter. Of the three so-called monastic graces, *Simplicitas, Benignitas, Hilaritas*, the last is not

A Home of the Silent Brotherhood

his. Even for necessary speech he is taught to substitute a language of signs, as fully systematized as the speech of the deaf and dumb. Should he, while at work, wound his fellow-workman, sorrow may be expressed by striking his breast. A desire to confess is shown by lifting one hand to the mouth and striking the breast with the other. The maker of cheese crosses two fingers at the middle point to let you know that it is made half of milk and half of cream. The guest-master, whose business it is to act as your guide through the abbey and the grounds, is warily mindful of his special functions and requests you to address none but him. Only the abbot is free to speak when and as his judgment may approve. It is silence, says the Trappist, that shuts out new ideas, worldly topics, controversy. It is silence that enables the soul to contemplate with singleness and mortification the infinite perfections of the Eternal.

In the abbey it is this pervasive hush that falls like a leaden pall upon the stranger who has rushed in from the talking universe. Are these priests modern survivals of the rapt solitaries of India? The days pass, and the world, which seemed in hailing distance to you at first, has receded to dim remoteness. You stand at the window of your room

A Home of the Silent Brotherhood

looking out, and hear in the autumn trees only the flute-like note of some migratory bird, passing slowly on towards the south. You listen within, and hear but a key turning in distant locks and the slow-retreating footsteps of some dusky figure returning to its lonely self-communings. The utmost precaution is taken to avoid noise; in the dormitory not even your guide will speak to you, but explains by gesture and signs. During the short siesta the Trappists allow themselves, if one of them, not wishing to sleep, gets permission to read in his so-called cell, he must turn the pages of his book inaudibly. In the refectory, while the meal is eaten and the appointed reader in the tribune goes through a service, if one through carelessness makes a noise by so much as dropping a fork or a spoon, he leaves his seat and prostrates himself on the floor until bidden by the superior to arise. The same penance is undergone in the church by any one who should distract attention with the clasp of his book.

A hard life, to purely human seeming, does the Trappist make for the body. He thinks nothing of it. It is his evil tenement of flesh, whose humors are an impediment to sanctification, whose propensities are to be kept down by the practice of austerities. To it in part his

A Home of the Silent Brotherhood

monastic vows are addressed—perpetual and utter poverty, chastity, manual labor, silence, seclusion, penance, obedience. The perfections and glories of his monastic state culminate in the complete abnegation and destruction of animal nature, and in the correspondence of his earthly life with the holiness of divine instruction. The war of the Jesuit is with the world; the war of the Trappist is with himself. From his narrow bed, on which are simply a coarse thin mattress, pillow, sheet, and coverlet, he rises at two o'clock, on certain days at one, on others yet at twelve. He has not undressed, but has slept in his daily garb, with the cincture around his waist.

This dress consists, if he be a brother, of the roughest dark-brown serge-like stuff, the over-garment of which is a long robe; if a Father, of a similar material, but white in color, the over-garment being the cowl, beneath which is the black scapular. He changes it only once in two weeks. The frequent use of the bath, as tending to luxuriousness, is forbidden him, especially if he be young. His diet is vegetables, fruit, honey, cider, cheese, and brown-bread. Only when sick or infirm may he take even fish or eggs. His table-service is pewter, plain earthenware, a heavy wooden spoon and fork of his own making, and the bottom of a

A Home of the Silent Brotherhood

broken bottle for a salt-cellar. If he wears the white cowl, he eats but one such frugal repast a day during part of the year; if the brown robe, and therefore required to do more work, he has besides this meal an early morning luncheon called "mixt." He renounces all claim to his own person, all right over his own powers. "I am as wax," he exclaims; "mould me as you will." By the law of his patron saint, if commanded to do things too hard, or even impossible, he must still undertake them.

For the least violations of the rules of his order; for committing a mistake while reciting a psalm, responsory, antiphon, or lesson; for giving out one note instead of another, or saying *dominus* instead of *domino;* for breaking or losing anything, or committing any fault while engaged in any kind of work in kitchen, pantry, bakery, garden, trade, or business—he must humble himself and make public satisfaction forthwith. Nay, more: each by his vows is forced to become his brother's keeper, and to proclaim him publicly in the community chapter for the slightest overt transgression. For charity's sake, however, he may not judge motives nor make vague general charges.

The Trappist does not walk beyond the en-

A Home of the Silent Brotherhood

closures except by permission. He must repress ineffably tender yearnings that visit and vex the human heart in this life. The death of the nearest kindred is not announced to him. Forgotten by the world, by him it is forgotten. Yet not wholly. When he lays the lashes of the scourge on his flesh—it may be on his carious bones—he does it not for his own sins alone, but for the sins of the whole world; and in his searching, self-imposed humiliations, there is a silent, broad out-reaching of sympathetic effort in behalf of all his kind. Sorrow may not depict itself freely on his face. If a suffering invalid, he must manifest no interest in the progress of his malady, feel no concern regarding the result. In his last hour, he sees ashes strewn upon the floor in the form of a cross, a thin scattering of straw made over them, and his body extended thereon to die; and from this hard bed of death he knows it will be borne on a bier by his brethren and laid in the grave without coffin or shroud.

VI

BUT who can judge such a life save him who has lived it? Who can say what undreamt-of spiritual compensations may not come even in this present time as a reward for bodily austerities? What fine realities may not body themselves forth to the eye of the soul, strained of grossness, steadied from worldly agitation, and taught to gaze year after year into the awfulness and mystery of its own being and deep destiny? "Monasticism," says Mr. Froude, "we believe to have been the realization of the infinite loveliness and beauty of personal purity; and the saint in the desert was the apotheosis of the spiritual man." However this may be, here at Gethsemane you see one of the severest expressions of its faith that the soul has ever given, either in ancient or in modern times; and you cease to think of these men as members of a religious order, in the study of them as exponents of a common humanity struggling with the problem of its rela-

A Home of the Silent Brotherhood

tion to the Infinite. One would wish to lay hold upon the latent elements of power and truth and beauty in their system which enables them to say with quiet cheerfulness, "We are happy, perfectly happy."

Excepting this ceaseless war between flesh and spirit, the abbey seems a peaceful place. Its relations with the outside world have always been kindly. During the Civil War it was undisturbed by the forces of each army. Food and shelter it has never denied even to the poorest, and it asks no compensation, accepting such as the stranger may give. The savor of good deeds extends beyond its walls, and near by is a free school under its control, where for more than a quarter of a century boys of all creeds have been educated.

There comes some late autumnal afternoon when you are to leave the place. With a strange feeling of farewell, you grasp the hands of those whom you have been given the privilege of knowing, and step slowly out past the meek sacristan, past the noiseless garden, past the porter's lodge and the misplaced rabbits, past the dim avenue of elms, past the great iron gateway, and, walking along the sequestered road until you have reached the summit of a wooded knoll half a mile away, turn and look back. Half a mile! The distance is infinite. The

A Home of the Silent Brotherhood

last rays of the sun seem hardly able to reach the pale cross on the spire which anon fades into the sky; and the monastery bell, that sends its mellow tones across the shadowy landscape, is rung from an immemorial past.

It is the hour of the *Compline*, the *Salve*, and the *Angelus*—the last of the seven services that the Trappist holds between two o'clock in the morning and this hour of early nightfall. Standing alone in the silent darkness you allow imagination to carry you once more into the church. You sit in one of the galleries and look down upon the stalls of the monks ranged along the walls of the nave. There is no light except the feeble gleam of a single low red cresset that swings ever-burning before the altar. You can just discern a long line of nameless dusky figures creep forth from the deeper gloom and glide noiselessly into their seats. You listen to the *cantus plenus gravitate*—those long, level notes with sorrowful cadences and measured pauses, sung by a full, unfaltering chorus of voices, old and young. It is the song that smote the heart of Bossuet with such sadness in the desert of Normandy two and a half centuries ago.

Anon by some unseen hand two tall candles are lighted on the altar. The singing is hushed. From the ghostly line of white-robed Fathers a shadowy figure suddenly moves towards

A Home of the Silent Brotherhood

the spot in the middle of the church where the bell-rope hangs, and with slow, weird movements rings the solemn bell until it fills the cold, gray arches with quivering sound. One will not in a lifetime forget the impressiveness of the scene—the long tapering shadows that stretch out over the dimly lighted, polished floor from this figure silhouetted against the brighter light from the altar beyond; the bowed, moveless forms of the monks in brown almost indiscernible in the gloom; the spectral glamour reflected from the robes of the bowed Fathers in white; the ghastly, suffering scene of the Saviour, strangely luminous in the glare of the tall candles. It is the daily climax in the devotions of the Old World monks at Gethsemane.

HOMESTEADS OF THE BLUE-GRASS

I

KENTUCKY is a land of rural homes. The people are out in the country with a perennial appetite and passion for the soil. Like Englishmen, they are by nature no dwellers in cities; like older Saxon forefathers, they have a strong feeling for a habitation even no better than a one-story log-house, with furniture of the rudest kind, and cooking in the open air, if, only, it be surrounded by a plot of ground and individualized by all-encompassing fences. They are gregarious at respectful distances, dear to them being that sense of personal worth and importance which comes from territorial aloofness, from domestic privacy, from a certain lordship over all they survey.

The land they hold has a singular charm and power of infusing fierce, tender desire of ownership. Centuries before it was possessed by them, all ruthless aboriginal wars for its sole occupancy had resolved themselves into the final understanding that it be wholly

Homesteads of the Blue-Grass

claimed by none. Bounty in land was the coveted reward of Virginia troops in the old French and Indian war. Hereditary love of land drew the earliest settlers across the perilous mountains. Rapacity for land caused them to rush down into the green plains, fall upon the natives, slay, torture, hack to pieces, and sacrifice wife and child, with the swift, barbaric hardihood and unappeasable fury of Northmen of old descending upon the softer shores of France. Acquisition of land was the determinative principle of the new civilization. Litigation concerning land has made famous the decisions of their courts of law. The surveyor's chain should be wrapped about the rifle as a symbolic epitome of pioneer history. It was for land that they turned from the Indians upon one another, and wrangled, cheated, and lied. They robbed Boone until he had none left in which to lay his bones. One of the first acts of one of the first colonists was to glut his appetite by the purchase of all of the State that lies south of the Kentucky River. The middle-class land-owner has always been the controlling element of population. To-day more of the people are engaged in agriculture than in all other pursuits combined; taste for it has steadily drawn a rich stream of younger generations hither and thither into the young-

Homesteads of the Blue-Grass

er West; and to-day, as always, the broad, average ideal of a happy life is expressed in the quiet holding of perpetual pastures. Steam, said Emerson, is almost an Englishman; grass is almost a Kentuckian. Wealth, labor, productions, revenues, public markets, public improvements, manners, characters, social modes — all speak in common of the country, and fix attention upon the soil. The staples attest the predominance of agriculture; unsurpassed breeds of stock imply the verdure of the woodlands; turnpikes, the finest on the continent, furnish viaducts for the garnered riches of the earth, and prove the high development of rural life, the every-day luxury of delightful riding and driving. Even the crow, the most boldly characteristic freebooter of the air, whose cawing is often the only sound heard in dead February days, or whose flight amid his multitudinous fellows forms long black lines across the morning and the evening sky, tells of fat pickings and profitable thefts in innumerable fields. In Kentucky a rustic young woman of Homeric sensibility might be allowed to discover in the slow-moving panorama of white clouds her father's herd of short-horned cattle grazing through heavenly pastures, and her lover to see in the halo around the moon a perfect celestial race-track.

Homesteads of the Blue-Grass

Comparatively weak and unpronounced are the features of urban life. The many little towns and villages scattered at easy distances over the State for the most part draw out a thin existence by reason of surrounding rural populations. They bear the pastoral stamp. Up to their very environs approach the cultivated fields, the meadows of brilliant green, the delicate woodlands; in and out along the white highways move the tranquil currents of rural trade; through their streets groan and creak the loaded wagons; on the sidewalks the most conspicuous human type is the owner of the soil. Once a month county-seats overflow with the incoming tide of country folk, livery stables are crowded with horses and vehicles, court-house squares become marketplaces for traffic in stock. But when emptied of country folk, they sink again into repose, all but falling asleep of summer noonings, and in winter seeming frost-locked with the outlying woods and streams.

Remarkable is the absence of considerable cities, there being but one that may be said truly to reflect Kentucky life, and that situated on the river frontier, a hundred miles from the center of the State. Think of it! A population of some two millions with only one interior town that contains over five thousand

Homesteads of the Blue-Grass

white inhabitants. Hence Kentucky makes no impression abroad by reason of its urban population. Lexington, Bowling Green, Harrodsburg, Winchester, Richmond, Frankfort, Mount Sterling, and all the others, where do they stand in the scale of American cities? Hence, too, the disparaging contrast liable to be drawn between Kentucky and the gigantic young States of the West. Where is the magnitude of the commonwealth, where the ground of the sense of importance in the people? No huge mills and gleaming forges, no din of factories and throb of mines, nowhere any colossal centres for rushing, multiform American energy. The answer must be: Judge the State thus far as an agricultural State; the people as an agricultural people. In time no doubt the rest will come. All other things are here, awaiting occasion and development. The eastern portions of the State now verge upon an era of long-delayed activity. There lie the mines, the building-stone, the illimitable wealth of timbers; there soon will be opened new fields for commercial and industrial centralization. But hitherto in Kentucky it has seemed enough that the pulse of life should beat with the heart of nature, and be in unison with the slow unfolding and decadence of the seasons. The farmer can go no

Homesteads of the Blue-Grass

faster than the sun, and is rich or poor by the law of planetary orbits. In all central Kentucky not a single village of note has been founded within three-quarters of a century, and some villages a hundred years old have not succeeded in gaining even from this fecund race more than a thousand or two thousand inhabitants. But these little towns are inaccessible to the criticism that would assault their commercial greatness. Business is not their boast. Sounded to its depths, the serene sea in which their existence floats will reveal a bottom, not of mercantile, but of social ideas; studied as to cost or comfort, the architecture in which the people have expressed themselves will appear noticeable, not in their business houses and public buildings, but in their homes. If these towns pique themselves pointedly on anything, it is that they are the centres of genial intercourse and polite entertainment. Even commercial Louisville must find its peculiar distinction in the number of its sumptuous private residences. It is wellnigh a rule that in Kentucky the value of the house is out of proportion to the value of the estate.

But if the towns regard themselves as the provincial fortresses of good society, they do not look down upon the home life of the coun-

Homesteads of the Blue-Grass

try. Between country and town in Kentucky exists a relation unique and well to be studied: such a part of the population of the town owning or managing estates in the country; such a part of the population of the country being business or professional men in town. For it is strikingly true that here all vocations and avocations of life may and do go with tillage, and there are none it is not considered to adorn. The first Governor of the State was awarded his domain for raising a crop of corn, and laid down public life at last to renew his companionship with the plough. "I retire," said Clay, many years afterwards, "to the shades of Ashland." The present Governor (1888), a man of large wealth, lives, when at home, iñ a rural log-house built near the beginning of the century. His predecessor in office was a farmer. Hardly a man of note in all the past or present history of the State but has had his near or immediate origin in the woods and fields. Formerly it was the custom—less general now —that young men should take their academic degrees in the colleges of the United States, sometimes in those of Europe, and, returning home, hang up their diplomas as votive offerings to the god of boundaries. To-day you will find the ex-minister to a foreign court spending his final years in the solitude of his

Homesteads of the Blue-Grass

farm-house, and the representative at Washington making his retreat to the restful homestead. The banker in town bethinks him of stocks at home that know no panic; the clergyman studies St. Paul amid the native corn, and muses on the surpassing beauty of David as he rides his favorite horse through green pastures and beside still waters.

Hence, to be a farmer here implies no social inferiority, no rusticity, no boorishness. Hence, so clearly interlaced are urban and rural society that there results a homogeneousness of manners, customs, dress, entertainments, ideals, and tastes. Hence, the infiltration of the country with the best the towns contain. More, indeed, than this: rather to the country than to the towns in Kentucky must one look for the local history of the home life. There first was implanted under English and Virginian influences the antique style of country-seat; there flourished for a time gracious manners that were the high-born endowment of the olden school; there in piquant contrast were developed side by side the democratic and aristocratic spirits, working severally towards equality and caste; there was established the State reputation for effusive private hospitalities; and there still are peculiarly cherished the fading traditions of more festive boards and

Homesteads of the Blue-Grass

kindlier hearthstones. If the feeling of the whole people could be interpreted by a single saying, it would perhaps be this : that whether in town or country—and if in the country, not remotely here or there, but in wellnigh unbroken succession from estate to estate—they have attained a notable stage in the civilization of the home. This is the common conviction, this the idol of the tribe. The idol itself may rest on the fact of provincial isolation, which is the fortress of self-love and neighborly devotion ; but it suffices for the present purpose to say that it is an idol still, worshipped for the divinity it is thought to enshrine. Hence, you may assail the Kentuckian on many grounds, and he will hold his peace. You may tell him that he has no great cities, that he does not run with the currents of national progress; but never tell him that the home life of his fellows and himself is not as good as the best in the land. Domesticity is the State porcupine, presenting an angry quill to every point of attack. To write of homes in Kentucky, therefore, and particularly of rural homes, is to enter the very citadel of the popular affections.

II

AT first they built for the tribe, working together like beavers in common cause against nature and their enemies. Home life and domestic architecture began among them with the wooden-fort community, the idea of which was no doubt derived from the frontier defences of Virginia, and modified by the Kentuckians with a view to domestic use. This building habit culminated in the erection of some two hundred rustic castles, the sites of which in some instances have been identified. It was a singularly fit sort of structure, adjusting itself desperately and economically to the necessities of environment. For the time society lapsed into a state which, but for the want of lords and retainers, was feudalism of the rudest kind. There were gates for sally and swift retreat, bastions for defence, and loopholes in cabin walls for deadly volleys. There were hunting-parties winding forth stealthily without horn or hound, and returning with

Homesteads of the Blue-Grass

game that would have graced the great feudal halls. There was siege, too, and suffering, and death enough, God knows, mingled with the lowing of cattle and the clatter of looms. Some morning, even, you might have seen a slight girl trip covertly out to the little cotton-patch in one corner of the enclosure, and, blushing crimson over the snowy cotton-bolls, pick the wherewithal to spin her bridal dress; for in these forts they married also and bore children. Many a Kentucky family must trace its origin through the tribal communities pent up within a stockade, and discover that the family plate consisted then of a tin cup, and, haply, an iron fork.

But, as soon as might be, this compulsory village life broke eagerly asunder into private homes. The common building form was that of the log-house. It is needful to distinguish this from the log-house of the mountaineer, which is found throughout eastern Kentucky to-day. Encompassed by all difficulties, the pioneer yet reared himself a better, more enduring habitation. One of these, still intact after the lapse of more than a century, stands as a singularly interesting type of its kind, and brings us face to face with primitive architecture. "Mulberry Hill," a double house, two and a half stories high, with a central hall, was built

Homesteads of the Blue-Grass

in Jefferson County, near Louisville, in 1785, for John Clark, the father of General George Rogers Clark.

The settlers made the mistake of supposing that the country lacked building-stone, so deep under the loam and verdure lay the whole foundation rock; but soon they discovered that their better houses had only to be taken from beneath their feet. The first stone house in the State, and withal the most notable, is "Traveller's Rest," in Lincoln County, built in 1783 by Governor Metcalf, who was then a stone-mason, for Isaac Shelby, the first Governor of Kentucky. To those who know the blue-grass landscape, this type of homestead is familiar enough, with its solidity of foundation, great thickness of walls, enormous, low chimneys, and little windows. The owners were the architects and builders, and with stern, necessitous industry translated their condition into their work, giving it an intensely human element. It harmonized with need, not with feeling; was built by the virtues, and not by the vanities. With no fine balance of proportion, with details few, scant, and crude, the entire effect of the architecture was not unpleasing, so honest was its poverty, so rugged and robust its purpose. It was the gravest of all historic commentaries written in stone. Varied fate has overtaken

Homesteads of the Blue-Grass

these old-time structures. Many have been torn down, yielding their well-chosen sites to newer, showier houses. Others became in time the quarters of the slaves. Others still have been hidden away beneath weather-boarding — a veneer of commonplace modernism — as though whitewashed or painted plank were finer than roughhewn graystone. But one is glad to discover that in numerous instances they are the preferred homes of those who have taste for the old in native history, and pride in family associations and traditions. On the thinned, open landscape nothing stands out with a more pathetic air of nakedness than one of these stone houses, long since abandoned and fallen into ruin. Under the Kentucky sky houses crumble and die without seeming to grow old, without an aged toning down of colors, without the tender memorials of mosses and lichens, and of the whole race of clinging things. So not until they are quite overthrown does Nature reclaim them, or draw once more to her bosom the walls and chimneys within whose faithful bulwarks, and by whose cavernous, glowing recesses, our great-grandmothers and great-grandfathers danced and made love, married, suffered, and fell asleep.

Neither to the house of logs, therefore, nor to that of stone must we look for the earliest

Homesteads of the Blue-Grass

embodiment of positive taste in domestic architecture. This found its first, and, considering the exigencies of the period, its most noteworthy expression in the homestead of brick. No finer specimen survives than that built in 1796, on a plan furnished by Thomas Jefferson to John Brown, who had been his law student, remained always his honored friend, and became one of the founders of the commonwealth. It is a rich landmark, this old manor-place on the bank of the Kentucky River, in Frankfort. The great hall with its pillared archway is wide enough for dancing the Virginia reel. The suites of high, spacious rooms; the carefully carved woodwork of the window-casings and the doors; the tall, quaint mantel-frames; the deep fireplaces with their shining fire-dogs and fenders of brass, brought laboriously enough on pack-mules from Philadelphia; the brass locks and keys; the portraits on the walls—all these bespeak the early implantation in Kentucky of a taste for sumptuous life and entertainment. The house is like a far-descending echo of colonial Old Virginia.

Famous in its day—for it is already beneath the sod—and built not of wood, nor of stone, nor of brick, but in part of all, was "Chaumière," the home of David Meade during the closing years of the last, and the early years of

Homesteads of the Blue-Grass

the present, century. The owner, a Virginian who had been much in England, brought back with him notions of the baronial style of country-seat, and in Jessamine County, some ten miles from Lexington, built a home that lingers in the mind like some picture of the imagination. It was a villa-like place, a cluster of rustic cottages, with a great park laid out in the style of Old World landscape-gardening. There were artificial rivers spanned by bridges, and lakes with islands crowned by temples. There were terraces and retired alcoves, and winding ways cut through flowering thickets. A fortune was spent on the grounds; a retinue of servants was employed in nurturing their beauty. The dining-room, wainscoted with walnut and relieved by deep window-seats, was rich with the family service of silver and glass; on the walls of other rooms hung family portraits by Thomas Hudson and Sir Joshua Reynolds. Two days in the week were appointed for formal receptions. There Jackson and Monroe and Taylor were entertained; there Aaron Burr was held for a time under arrest; there the old school showed itself in buckles and knee-breeches, and rode abroad in a yellow chariot with outriders in blue cloth and silver buttons.

Near Lexington may be found a further not-

Homesteads of the Blue-Grass

able example of early architecture in the Todd homestead, the oldest house in the region, built by the brother of John Todd, who was Governor of Kentucky Territory, including Illinois. It is a strong, spacious brick structure reared on a high foundation of stone, with a large, square hall and square rooms in suites, connected by double doors. To the last century also belongs the low, irregular pile that became the Wickliffe, and later the Preston, house in Lexington—a striking example of the taste then prevalent for plain, or even commonplace, exteriors, if combined with interiors that touched the imagination with the suggestion of something stately and noble and courtly.

There are few types of homes erected in the last century. The wonder is not that such places exist, but that they should have been found in Kentucky at such a time. For society had begun as the purest of democracies. Only a little while ago the people had been shut up within a stockade. Stress of peril and hardship had levelled the elements of population to more than a democracy: it had knit them together as one endangered human brotherhood. Hence the sudden, fierce flaring up of sympathy with the French Revolution; hence the deep re-echoing war-cry of Jacobin emissaries. But

Homesteads of the Blue-Grass

scarcely had the wave of primitive conquest flowed over the land, and wealth followed in its peaceful wake, before life fell apart into the extremes of social caste. The memories of former position, the influences of old domestic habits were powerful still ; so that, before a generation passed, Kentucky society gave proof of the continuity of its development from Virginia. The region of the James River, so rich in antique homesteads, began to renew itself in the region of the blue-grass. On a new and larger canvas began to be painted the picture of shaded lawns, wide portals, broad staircases, great halls, drawing-rooms, and dining-rooms, wainscoting, carved wood-work, and waxed hard-wood floors. In came a few yellow chariots, morocco-lined, and drawn by four horses. In came the powder, the wigs, and the queues, the ruffled shirts, the knee-breeches, the glittering buckles, the high-heeled slippers, and the frosty brocades. Over the Alleghanies, in slow-moving wagons, came the massive mahogany furniture, the sunny brasswork, the tall silver candlesticks, the nervous-looking, thin legged little pianos. In came old manners and old speech and old prides : the very Past gathered together its household gods and made an exodus into the Future.

Without due regard to these essential facts

Homesteads of the Blue-Grass

the social system of the State must ever remain poorly understood. Hitherto they have been but little considered. To the popular imagination the most familiar type of the early Kentuckian is that of the fighter, the hunter, the rude, heroic pioneer and his no less heroic wife : people who left all things behind them and set their faces westward, prepared to be new creatures if such they could become. But on the dim historic background are the stiff figures of another type, people who were equally bent on being old-fashioned creatures if such they could remain. Thus, during the final years of the last century and the first quarter of the present one, Kentucky life was richly overlaid with ancestral models. Closely studied, the elements of population by the close of this period somewhat resembled a landed gentry, a robust yeomanry, a white tenantry, and a black peasantry. It was only by degrees—by the dying out of the fine old types of men and women, by longer absence from the old environment and closer contact with the new—that society lost its inherited and acquired its native characteristics, or became less Virginian and more Kentuckian. Gradually, also, the white tenantry waned and the black peasantry waxed. The aristocratic spirit, in becoming more Kentuckian, unbent somewhat its pride, and the

Homesteads of the Blue-Grass

democratic, in becoming more Kentuckian, took on a pride of its own; so that when social life culminated with the first half-century, there had been produced over the Blue-grass Region, by the intermingling of the two, that widely diffused and peculiar type which may be described as an aristocratic democracy, or a democratic aristocracy, according to one's choosing of a phrase. The beginnings of Kentucky life represented not simply a slow development from the rudest pioneer conditions, but also a direct and immediate implantation of the best of long-established social forms. And in nowise did the latter embody itself more persuasively and lastingly than in the building of costly homes.

III

WITH the opening of the present century, that taste had gone on developing. A specimen of early architecture in the style of the old English mansion is to be found in "Locust Grove," a massive and enduring structure—not in the Blue-grass Region, it is true, but several miles from Louisville—built in 1800 for Colonel Croghan, brother-in-law of General George Rogers Clark; and still another remains in "Spring Hill," in Woodford County, the home of Nathaniel Hart, who had been a boy in the fort at Boonesborough. Until recently a further representative, though remodelled in later times, survived in the Thompson place at "Shawnee Springs," in Mercer County.

Consider briefly the import of such country homes as these — "Traveller's Rest," "Chaumière," "Spring Hill," and "Shawnee Springs." Built remotely here and there, away from the villages or before villages were formed, in a

Homesteads of the Blue-Grass

country not yet traversed by limestone highways or even by lanes, they, and such as they, were the beacon-lights, many-windowed and kind, of Kentucky entertainment. "Traveller's Rest" was on the great line of emigration from Abingdon through Cumberland Gap. Its roof-tree was a boon of universal shelter, its very name a perpetual invitation to all the weary. Long after the country became thickly peopled it, and such places as it, remained the rallying-points of social festivity in their several counties, or drew their guests from remoter regions. They brought in the era of hospitalities, which by-and-by spread through the towns and over the land. If one is ever to study this trait as it flowered to perfection in Kentucky life, one must look for it in the society of some fifty years ago. Then horses were kept in the stables, servants were kept in the halls. Guests came uninvited, unannounced; tables were regularly set for surprises. "Put a plate," said an old Kentuckian of the time with a large family connection—"always put a plate for the last one of them down to the youngest grandchild." What a Kentuckian would have thought of being asked to come on the thirteenth of the month and to leave on the twentieth, it is difficult to imagine. The wedding-presents of brides were

Homesteads of the Blue-Grass

not only jewels and silver and gold, but a round of balls. The people were laughed at for their too impetuous civilities. In whatever quarter of the globe they should happen to meet for the hour a pleasing stranger, they would say in parting, "And when you come to Kentucky, be certain to come to my house."

Yet it is needful to discriminate, in speaking of Kentucky hospitality. Universally gracious towards the stranger, and quick to receive him for his individual worth, within the State hospitality ran in circles, and the people turned a piercing eye on one another's social positions. If in no other material aspect did they embody the history of descent so sturdily as in the building of homes, in no other trait of home life did they reflect this more clearly than in family pride. Hardly a little town but had its classes that never mingled; scarce a rural neighborhood but insisted on the sanctity of its salt-cellar and the gloss of its mahogany. The spirit of caste was somewhat Persian in its gravity. Now the Alleghanies were its background, and the heroic beginnings of Kentucky life supplied its warrant; now it overleaped the Alleghanies, and allied itself to the memories of deeds and names in older States. But if some professed to look down,

Homesteads of the Blue-Grass

none professed to look up. Deference to an upper class, if deference existed, was secret and resentful, not open and servile. The history of great political contests in the State is largely the victory and defeat of social types. Herein lies a difficulty: you touch any point of Kentucky life, and instantly about it cluster antagonisms and contradictions. The false is true; the true is false. Society was aristocratic; it was democratic; it was neither; it was both. There was intense family pride, and no family pride. The ancestral sentiment was weak, and it was strong. 'To-day you will discover the increasing vogue of an *heraldica Kentuckiensis*, and to-day an absolute disregard of a distinguished past. One tells but partial truths.

Of domestic architecture in a brief and general way something has been said. The prevailing influence was Virginian, but in Lexington and elsewhere may be observed evidences of French ideas in the glasswork and designs of doors and windows, in rooms grouped around a central hall with arching niches and alcoves; for models made their way from New Orleans as well as from the East. Out in the country, however, at such places as those already mentioned, and in homes nearer town, as at Ashland, a purely English taste was sometimes

Homesteads of the Blue-Grass

shown for woodland parks with deer, and, what was more peculiarly Kentuckian, elk and buffalo. This taste, once so conspicuous, has never become extinct, and certainly the landscape is receptive enough to all such stately purposes. At "Spring Hill" and elsewhere, to-day, one may stroll through woods that have kept a touch of their native wildness. There was the English love of lawns, too, with a low matted green turf and wide-spreading shade-trees above—elm and maple, locust and poplar—the English fondness for a home half hidden with evergreens and creepers and shrubbery, to be approached by a leafy avenue, a secluded gate-way, and a gravelled drive; for highways hardly admit to the heart of rural life in Kentucky, and way-side homes, to be dusted and gazed at by every passer-by, would little accord with the spirit of the people. This feeling of family seclusion and completeness also portrayed itself very tenderly in the custom of family graveyards, which were in time to be replaced by the democratic cemetery; and no one has ever lingered around those quiet spots of aged and drooping cedars, fast-fading violets, and perennial myrtle, without being made to feel that they grew out of the better heart and fostered the finer senses.

Another evidence of culture among the first

Homesteads of the Blue-Grass

generations of Kentuckians is to be seen in the private collections of portraits, among which one wanders now with a sort of stricken feeling that the higher life of Kentucky in this regard never went beyond its early promise. Look into the meagre history of native art, and you will discover that nearly all the best work belongs to this early time. It was possible then that a Kentuckian could give up law and turn to painting. Almost in the wilderness Jouett created rich, luminous, startling canvases. Artists came from older States to sojourn and to work, and were invited or summoned from abroad. Painting was taught in Lexington in 1800. Well for Jouett, perhaps, that he lived when he did; better for Hart, perhaps, that he was not born later; they might have run for Congress. One is prone to recur time and again to this period, when the ideals of Kentucky life were still wavering or unformed, and when there was the greatest receptivity to outside impressions. Thinking of social life as it was developed, say in and around Lexington—of artists coming and going, of the statesmen, the lecturers, the lawyers, of the dignity and the energy of character, of the intellectual dinners—one is inclined to liken the local civilization to a truncated cone, to a thing that should have towered to a

Homesteads of the Blue-Grass

symmetric apex, but somehow has never risen very high above a sturdy base.

But to speak broadly of home life after it became more typically Kentuckian, and after architecture began to reflect with greater uniformity the character of the people. And here one can find material comfort, if not æsthetic delight ; for it is the whole picture of human life in the Blue-grass Region that pleases. Ride east and west, or north and south, along highway or by-way, and the picture is the same. One almost asks for relief from the monotony of a merely well-to-do existence, almost sighs for the extremes of squalor and splendor, that nowhere may be seen, and that would seem out of place if anywhere confronted. On, and on, and on you go, seeing only the repetition of field and meadow, wood and lawn, a winding stream, an artificial pond, a sunny vineyard, a blooming orchard, a stone-wall, a hedge-row, a tobacco barn, a warehouse, a race-track, cattle under the trees, sheep on the slopes, swine in the pools, and, half hidden by evergreens and shrubbery, the homelike, unpretentious houses that crown very simply and naturally the entire picture of material prosperity. They strike you as built not for their own sakes. Few will offer anything that lays hold upon the memory, unless it be per-

Homesteads of the Blue-Grass

haps a front portico with Doric, Ionic, or Corinthian columns; for the typical Kentuckian likes to go into his house through a classic entrance, no matter what inharmonious things may be beyond; and after supper on summer evenings nothing fills him with serener comfort than to tilt his chair back against a classic support, as he smokes a pipe and argues on the immortality of a pedigree.

On the whole, one feels that nature has long waited for a more exquisite sense in domestic architecture; that the immeasurable possibilities of delightful landscape have gone unrecognized or wasted. Too often there is in form and outline no harmony with the spirit of the scenery, and there is dissonance of color—color which makes the first and strongest impression. The realm of taste is prevailingly the realm of the want of taste, or of its meretricious and commonplace violations. Many of the houses have a sort of featureless, cold, insipid ugliness, and interior and exterior decorations are apt to go for nothing or for something worse. You repeat that nature awaits more art, since she made the land so kind to beauty; for no transformation of a rude, ungenial landscape is needed. The earth does not require to be trimmed and combed and perfumed. The airy vistas and delicate slopes

Homesteads of the Blue-Grass

are ready-made, the park-like woodlands invite, the tender, clinging children of the summer, the deep, echoless repose of the whole land, all ask that art be laid on every undulation and stored in every nook. And there are days with such Arcadian colors in air and cloud and sky —days with such panoramas of calm, sweet pastoral groups and harmonies below, such rippling and flashing of waters through green underlights and golden interspaces, that the shy, coy spirit of beauty seems to be wandering half sadly abroad and shunning all the haunts of man.

But little agricultural towns are not art-centres. Of itself rural life does not develop æsthetic perceptions, and the last, most difficult thing to bring into the house is this shy, elusive spirit of beauty. The Kentucky woman has perhaps been corrupted in childhood by tasteless surroundings. Her lovable mission, the creation of a multitude of small, lovely objects, is undertaken feebly and blindly. She may not know how to create beauty, may not know what beauty is. The temperament of her lord, too, is practical : a man of substance and stomach, sound at heart, and with an abiding sense of his own responsibility and importance, honestly insisting on sweet butter and new-laid eggs, home-made bread and home-

Homesteads of the Blue-Grass

grown mutton, but little revelling in the delicacies of sensibility, and with no more eye for crimson poppies or blue corn-flowers in his house than amid his grain. Many a Kentucky woman would make her home beautiful if her husband would allow her to do it.

Amid a rural people, also, no class of citizens is more influential than the clergy, who go about as the shepherds of the right; and without doubt in Kentucky, as elsewhere, ministerial ideals have wrought their effects on taste in architecture. Perhaps it is well to state that this is said broadly, and particularly of the past. The Kentucky preachers during earlier times were a fiery, zealous, and austere set, proclaiming that this world was not a home, but wilderness of sin, and exhorting their people to live under the awful shadow of Eternity. Beauty in every material form was a peril, the seductive garment of the devil. Well-nigh all that made for æsthetic culture was put down, and, like frost on venturesome flowers, sermons fell on beauty in dress, entertainment, equipage, houses, church architecture, music, the drama, the opera—everything. The meek young spirit was led to the creek or pond, and perhaps the ice was broken for her baptism. If, as she sat in the pew, any vision of her chaste loveliness reached the pulpit,

Homesteads of the Blue-Grass

back came the warning that she would some day turn into a withered hag, and must inevitably be "eaten of worms." What wonder if the sense of beauty pined or went astray and found itself completely avenged in the building of such churches? And yet there is nothing that even religion more surely demands than the fostering of the sense of beauty within us, and through this also we work towards the civilization of the future.

IV.

MANY rural homes have been built since the war, but the old type of country life has vanished. On the whole, there has been a strong movement of population towards the towns, rapidly augmenting their size. Elements of showiness and freshness have been added to their once unobtrusive architecture. And, in particular, that art movement and sudden quickening of the love of beauty which swept over this country a few years since has had its influence here. But for the most part the newer homes are like the newer homes in other American cities, and the style of interior appointment and decoration has few native characteristics. As a rule the people love the country life less than of yore, since an altered social system has deprived it of much leisure, and has added hardships. The Kentuckian does not regard it as part of his mission in life to feed fodder to stock; and servants are hard to get, the colored ladies and

Homesteads of the Blue-Grass

gentlemen having developed a taste for urban society.

What is to be the future of the Blue-grass Region? When population becomes denser and the pressure is felt in every neighborhood, who will possess it? One seems to see in certain tendencies of American life the probable answer to this question. The small farmer will be bought out, and will disappear. Estates will grow fewer and larger. The whole land will pass into the hands of the rich, being too precious for the poor to own. Already here and there one notes the disposition to create vast domains by the slow swallowing up of contiguous small ones. Consider in this connection the taste already shown by the rich American in certain parts of the United States to found a country-place in the style of an English lord. Consider, too, that the landscape is much like the loveliest of rural England; that the trees, the grass, the sculpture of the scenery are such as make the perfect beauty of a park; that the fox, the bob-white, the thoroughbred, and the deer are indigenous. Apparently, therefore, one can foresee the distant time when this will become the region of splendid homes and estates that will nourish a taste for out-door sports and offer an escape from the too-wearying cities. On the other

Homesteads of the Blue-Grass

hand, a powerful and ever-growing interest is that of the horse, racer or trotter. He brings into the State his increasing capital, his types of men. Year after year he buys farms, and lays out tracks, and builds stables, and edits journals, and turns agriculture into grazing. In time the Blue-grass Region may become the Yorkshire of America.

But let the future have its own. The country will become theirs who deserve it, whether they build palaces or barns. Only one hopes that when the old homesteads have been torn down or have fallen into ruins, the tradition may still run that they, too, had their day and deserved their page of history.

THROUGH CUMBERLAND GAP
ON HORSEBACK

1

FRESH fields lay before us that summer of 1885. We had left the rich, rolling plains of the Blue-grass Region in central Kentucky and set our faces towards the great Appalachian uplift on the south-eastern border of the State. There Cumberland Gap, that highswung gateway through the mountain, abides as a landmark of what Nature can do when she wishes to give an opportunity to the human race in its migrations and discoveries, without surrendering control of its liberty and its fate. It can never be too clearly understood by those who are wont to speak of "the Kentuckians" that this State has within its boundaries two entirely distinct elements of population—elements distinct in England before they came hither, distinct during more than a century of residence here, and distinct now in all that goes to constitute a separate community—occupations, manners and customs, dress, views of life, civilization. It is but a short distance from the

Through Cumberland Gap on Horseback

blue-grass country to the eastern mountains; but in traversing it you detach yourself from all that you have ever experienced, and take up the history of English-speaking men and women at the point it had reached a hundred or a hundred and fifty years ago.

Leaving Lexington, then, which is in the midst of the blue-grass plateau, we were come to Burnside, where begin the navigable waters of the Cumberland River, and the foot-hills of the Cumberland Mountains.

Burnside is not merely a station, but a mountain watering-place. The water is mostly in the bed of the river. We had come hither to get horses and saddle-bags, but to no purpose. The hotel was a sort of transition point between the civilization we had left and the primitive society we were to enter. On the veranda were some distinctly modern and conventional red chairs; but a green and yellow gourd-vine, carefully trained so as to shut out the landscape, was a genuine bit of local color. Under the fine beeches in the yard was swung a hammock, but it was made of boards braced between ropes, and was covered with a weather-stained piece of tarpaulin. There were electric bells in the house that did not electrify; and near the front entrance three barrels of Irish potatoes, with the tops off, spoke for themselves in the ab-

OLD FERRY AT POINT BURNSIDE

Through Cumberland Gap on Horseback

sence of the bill of fare. After supper, the cook, a tall, blue-eyed, white fellow, walked into my room without explanation, and carried away his guitar, showing that he had been wont to set his sighs to music in that quarter of the premises. The moon hung in that part of the heavens, and no doubt ogled him into many a midnight frenzy. Sitting under a beech-tree in the morning, I had watched a child from some city, dressed in white and wearing a blue ribbon around her goldenish hair, amuse herself by rolling old barrels (potato barrels probably, and she may have had a motive) down the hill-side and seeing them dashed to pieces on the railway track below. By-and-by some of the staves of one fell in, the child tumbled in also, and they all rolled over together. Upon the whole, it was an odd overlapping of two worlds. When the railway was first opened through this region a young man established a fruit store at one of the stations, and as part of his stock laid in a bunch of bananas. One day a mountaineer entered. Arrangements generally struck him with surprise, but everything else was soon forgotten in an adhesive contemplation of that mighty aggregation of fruit. Finally he turned away with this comment: "Damn me if them ain't the damnedest beans *I* ever seen!"

The scenery around Burnside is beautiful,

Through Cumberland Gap on Horseback

and the climate bracing. In the valleys was formerly a fine growth of walnut, but the principal timbers now are oak, ash, and sycamore, with yellow pine. I heard of a wonderful walnut tree formerly standing, by hiring vehicles to go and see which the owner of a livery-stable made three hundred and fifty dollars. Six hundred were offered for it on the spot. The hills are filled with the mountain limestone—that Kentucky oolite of which the new Cotton Exchange in New York is built. Here was Burnside's depot of supplies during the war, and here passed the great road—made in part a corduroy road at his order—from Somerset, Kentucky, to Jacksborough, over which countless stores were taken from central Kentucky and regions farther north into Tennessee. Supplies were brought up the river in small steamboats or overland in wagons, and when the road grew impassable, pack-mules were used. Sad sights there were in those sad days: the carcasses of animals at short intervals from here to Knoxville, and now and then a mule sunk up to his body in mire, and abandoned, with his pack on, to die. Here were batteries planted and rifle-pits dug, the vestiges of which yet remain; but where the forest timbers were then cut down a vigorous new growth has long been reclaiming the earth to native wildness, and altogether the

Through Cumberland Gap on Horseback

aspect of the place is peaceful and serene. Doves were flying in and out of the corn-fields on the hill-sides; there were green stretches in the valleys where cattle were grazing; and these, together with a single limestone road that wound upward over a distant ridge, recalled the richer scenes of the blue-grass lands.

Assured that we should find horses and saddle-bags at Cumberland Falls, we left Burnside in the afternoon, and were soon set down at a station some fifteen miles farther along, where a hack conveyed us to another of those mountain watering-places that are being opened up in various parts of eastern Kentucky for the enjoyment of a people that has never cared to frequent in large numbers the Atlantic seaboard.

As we drove on, the darkness was falling, and the scenery along the road grew wilder and grander. A terrific storm had swept over these heights, and the great trees lay uptorn and prostrate in every direction, or reeled and fell against each other like drunken giants—a scene of fearful elemental violence. On the summits one sees the tan-bark oak; lower down, the white oak; and lower yet, fine specimens of yellow poplar; while from the valleys to the crests is a dense and varied undergrowth, save where the ground has been burned

Through Cumberland Gap on Horseback

over, year after year, to kill it out and improve the grazing. Twenty miles to the south-east we had seen through the pale-tinted air the waving line of Jellico Mountains in Tennessee. Away to the north lay the Beaver Creek and the lower Cumberland, while in front of us rose the craggy, scowling face of Anvil Rock, commanding a view of Kentucky, Tennessee, and Virginia. The utter silence and heart-oppressing repose of primeval nature was around us. The stark white and gray trunks of the immemorial forest dead linked us to an inviolable past. The air seemed to blow upon us from over regions illimitable and unexplored, and to be fraught with unutterable suggestions. The full-moon swung itself aloft over the sharp touchings of the green with spectral pallor; and the evening-star stood lustrous on the western horizon in depths of blue as cold as a sky of Landseer, except where brushed by tremulous shadows of rose on the verge of the sunlit world. A bat wheeled upward in fantastic curves out of his undiscovered glade. And the soft tinkle of a single cow-bell far below marked the invisible spot of some lonely human habitation. By-and-by we lost sight of the heavens altogether, so dense and interlaced the forest. The descent of the hack appeared to be into a steep abyss of gloom; then all at

Through Cumberland Gap on Horseback

once we broke from the edge of the woods into a flood of moonlight; at our feet were the whirling, foaming rapids of the river; in our ears was the roar of the cataract, where the bow-crowned mist rose and floated upward and away in long trailing shapes of ethereal lightness.

The Cumberland River throws itself over the rocks here with a fall of seventy feet, or a perpendicular descent of sixty-two, making a mimic but beautiful Niagara. Just below, at Eagle Falls, it drops over its precipice in a lawny cascade. The roar of the cataract, under favorable conditions, may be heard up and down stream a distance of ten or twelve miles. You will not find in mountainous Kentucky a more picturesque spot.

While here, we had occasion to extend our acquaintance with native types. Two young men came to the hotel, bringing a bag of small, hard peaches to sell. Slim, slab-sided, stomachless, and serene, mild, and melancholy, they might have been lotos-eaters, only the suggestion of poetry was wanting. Their unutterable content came not from the lotos, but from their digestion. If they could sell their peaches, they would be happy; if not, they would be happy. What they could not sell, they could as well eat; and since no bargain

Through Cumberland Gap on Horseback

was made on this occasion, they took chairs on the hotel veranda, opened the bag, and fell to. I talked with the Benjamin of his tribe:
"Is that a good 'coon dog?"
"A mighty good 'coon dog. I hain't never seed him whipped by a varmint yit."
"Are there many 'coons in this country?"
"Several 'coons."
"Is this a good year for 'coons?"
"A mighty good year for 'coons. The woods is full o' varmints."
"Do 'coons eat corn?"
"'Coons is bad as hogs on corn, when they git tuk to it."
"Are there many wild turkeys in this country?"
"Several wild turkeys."
"Have you ever caught many 'coons?"
"I've cotched high as five 'coons out o' one tree."
"Are there many foxes in this country?"
"Several foxes."
"What's the best way to cook a 'coon?"
"Ketch him and parbile him, and then put him in cold water and soak him, and then put him in and bake him."
"Are there many hounds in this country?"
"Several hounds."
Here, among other discoveries, was a lin-

Through Cumberland Gap on Horseback

guistic one—the use of "several" in the sense of a great many, probably an innumerable multitude, as in the case of the 'coons. They hung around the hotel for hours, as beings utterly exempt from all the obligations and other phenomena of time.

"Why should we only toil, the roof and crown of things?"

The guide bespoken the evening before had made arrangements for our ride of some eighteen miles—was it not forty?—to Williamsburg, and in the afternoon made his appearance with three horses. Of these one was a mule, with a strong leaning towards his father's family. Of the three saddles one was a side-saddle, and another was an army saddle with refugee stirrups. The three beasts wore among them some seven shoes. My own mincing jade had none. Her name must have been Helen of Troy (all horses are named in Kentucky), so long ago had her great beauty disappeared. She partook with me of the terror which her own movements inspired; and if there ever was a well-defined case in which the man should have carried the beast, this was the one. While on her back I occasionally apologized for the injustice of riding her by handing her some sour

Through Cumberland Gap on Horseback

apples, the like of which she appeared never to have tasted before, just as it was told me she had never known the luxury of wearing shoes. It is often true that the owner of a horse in this region is too poor or too mean to have it shod.

Our route from Cumberland Falls lay through what is called "Little Texas," in Whitley County—a wilderness some twenty miles square. I say route, because there was not always a road; but for the guide, there would not always have been a direction. Rough as the country appears to one riding through it on horseback, it is truly called "flat woods country"; and viewed from Jellico Mountains, whence the local elevations are of no account, it looks like one vast sweep of sloping, densely wooded land. Here one may see noble specimens of yellow poplar in the deeper soil at the head of the ravines; pin-oak, and gum and willow, and the rarely beautiful wild-cucumber. Along the streams in the lowlands blooms the wild calacanthus, filling the air with fragrance, and here in season the wild camellia throws open its white and purple splendors.

It was not until we had passed out of "Little Texas" and reached Williamsburg, had gone thence to Barbourville, the county-seat of the adjoining county of Knox, and thence again

Through Cumberland Gap on Horseback

into Bell County, that we stopped at an old way-side inn on the Wilderness road from Kentucky through Cumberland Gap. Around us were the mountains—around us the mountaineers whom we wished to study.

II

STRAIGHT, slim, angular, white bodies; average or even unusual stature, without great muscular robustness; features regular and colorless; unanimated but intelligent; in the men sometimes fierce; in the women often sad; among the latter occasional beauty of a pure Greek type; a manner shy and deferential, but kind and fearless; eyes with a slow, long look of mild inquiry, or of general listlessness, or of unconscious and unaccountable melancholy; the key of life a low minor strain, losing itself in reverie; voices monotonous in intonation; movements uninformed by nervousness—these are characteristics of the Kentucky mountaineers. Living to-day as their forefathers lived a hundred years ago; hearing little of the world, caring nothing for it; responding feebly to the influences of civilization near the highways of travel in and around the towns, and latterly along the lines of railway communication; but sure to live here, if unin-

NATIVE TYPES

Through Cumberland Gap on Horseback

vaded and unaroused, in the same condition for a hundred years to come; lacking the spirit of development from within; devoid of sympathy with that boundless and ungovernable activity which is carrying the Saxon race in America from one state to another, whether better or worse. The origin of these people, the relation they sustain to the different population of the central Kentucky region—in fine, an account of them from the date of their settling in these mountains to the present time, when, as it seems, they are on the point of losing their isolation, and with it their distinctiveness—would imprison phases of life and character valuable alike to the special history of this country and to the general history of the human mind.

The land in these mountains is all claimed, but it is probably not all covered by actual patent. As evidence, a company has been formed to speculate in lands not secured by title. The old careless way of marking off boundaries by going from tree to tree, by partly surveying and partly guessing, explains the present uncertainty. Many own land by right of occupancy, there being no other claim. The great body of the people live on and cultivate little patches which they either own, or hold free, or pay rent for with a third of the

Through Cumberland Gap on Horseback

crop. These not unfrequently get together and trade farms as they would horses, no deed being executed. There is among them a mobile element—squatters—who make a hill-side clearing and live on it as long as it remains productive; then they move elsewhere. This accounts for the presence throughout the country of abandoned cabins, around which a new forest growth is springing up. Leaving out of consideration the few instances of substantial prosperity, the most of the people are abjectly poor, and they appear to have no sense of accumulation. The main crops raised are corn and potatoes. In the scant gardens will be seen patches of cotton, sorghum, and tobacco; flax also, though less than formerly. Many make insufficient preparation for winter, laying up no meat, but buying a piece of bacon now and then, and paying for it with work. In some regions the great problem of life is to raise two dollars and a half during the year for county taxes. Being pauper counties, they are exempt from State taxation. Jury fees are highly esteemed and much sought after. The manufacture of illicit mountain whiskey—"moonshine"—was formerly, as it is now, a considerable source of revenue; and a desperate sub-source of revenue from the same business has been the betrayal of its hidden places.

Through Cumberland Gap on Horseback

There is nothing harder or more dangerous to find now in the mountains than a still. Formerly digging "sang," as they call ginseng, was a general occupation. For this China was a great market. It has nearly all been dug out except in the wildest parts of the country, where entire families may still be seen "out sangin'." They took it into the towns in bags, selling it at a dollar and ten cents—perhaps a dollar and a half—a pound. This was mainly the labor of the women and the children, who went to work barefooted, amid briers and chestnut burs, copperheads and rattlesnakes. Indeed, the women prefer to go barefooted, finding shoes a trouble and constraint. It was a sad day for the people when the "sang" grew scarce. A few years ago one of the counties was nearly depopulated in consequence of a great exodus into Arkansas, whence had come the news that "sang" was plentiful. Not long since, during a season of scarcity in corn, a local store-keeper told the people of a county to go out and gather all the mandrake or "May-apple" root they could find. At first only the women and children went to work, the men holding back with ridicule. By-and-by they also took part, and that year some fifteen tons were gathered, at three cents a pound, and the whole country

Through Cumberland Gap on Horseback

thus got its seed-corn. Wild ginger was another root formerly much dug ; also to less extent "golden-seal" and "bloodroot." The sale of feathers from a few precarious geese helps to eke out subsistence. Their methods of agriculture—if methods they may be styled—are the most primitive. Ploughing is commonly done with a "bull-tongue," an implement hardly more than a sharpened stick with a metal rim; this is often drawn by an ox, or a half-yoke. But one may see women ploughing with two oxen. Traces are made of hickory or papaw, as also are bed-cords. Ropes are made of lynn bark. In some counties there is not so much as a fanning-mill, grain being winnowed by pouring it from basket to basket, after having been threshed with a flail, which is a hickory withe some seven feet long. Their threshing-floor is a clean place on the ground, and they take up grain, gravel, and dirt together, not knowing, or not caring for, the use of a sieve.

The grain is ground at their homes in a hand tub-mill, or one made by setting the nether millstone in a bee-gum, or by cutting a hole in a puncheon-log and sinking the stone into it. There are, however, other kinds of mills : the primitive little water-mill, which may be considered almost characteristic of this region ; in a few places improved water-mills, and small

Through Cumberland Gap on Horseback

steam-mills. It is the country of mills, farmhouses being furnished with one as with coffeepot or spinning-wheel. A simpler way of preparing corn for bread than by even the hand-mill is used in the late summer and early autumn, while the grain is too hard for eating as roasting-ears, and too soft to be ground in a mill. On a board is tacked a piece of tin through which holes have been punched from the under side, and over this tin the ears are rubbed, producing a coarse meal, of which "gritted bread" is made. Much pleasure and much health they get from their "gritted bread," which is sweet and wholesome for a hungry man.

Where civilization has touched on the highways and the few improved mills have been erected, one may see women going to mill with their scant sacks of grain, riding on a jack, a jennet, or a bridled ox. But this is not so bad as in North Carolina, where, Europa-like, they ride on bulls.

Aside from such occupations, the men have nothing to do—a little work in the spring, and nine months' rest. They love to meet at the country groceries and cross-roads, to shoot matches for beef, turkeys, or liquor, and to gamble. There is with them a sort of annual succession of amusements. In its season they

Through Cumberland Gap on Horseback

have the rage for pitching horse-shoes, the richer ones using dollar pieces. In consequence of their abundant leisure, the loneliness of the mountains, and their bravery and vigor, quarrels are frequent and feuds deadly. Personal enmities soon serve to array entire families in an attitude of implacable hostility; and in the course of time relatives and friends take sides, and a war of extermination ensues. The special origins of these feuds are various: blood heated and temper lost under the influence of "moonshine"; reporting the places and manufacturers of this; local politics; the survival of resentments engendered during the Civil War. These, together with all causes that lie in the passions of the human heart and spring from the constitution of all human society, often make the remote and insulated life of these people turbulent, reckless, and distressing.

But while thus bitter and cruel towards each other, they present to strangers the aspect of a polite, kind, unoffending, and most hospitable race. They will divide with you shelter and warmth and food, however scant, and will put themselves to trouble for your convenience with an unreckoning, earnest friendliness and good-nature that is touching to the last degree. No sham, no pretence; a true friend, or an open enemy. Of late they have had much

Through Cumberland Gap on Horseback

occasion to regard new-comers with distrust, which, once aroused, is difficult to dispel; and now they will wish to know you and your business before treating you with that warmth which they are only too glad to show.
The women do most of the work. From the few sheep, running wild, which the farm may own, they take the wool, which is carded, reeled, spun, and woven into fabrics by their own hands and on their rude implements. One or two spinning-wheels will be found in every house. Cotton from their little patches they clean by using a primitive hand cotton-gin. Flax, much spun formerly, is now less used. It is surprising to see from what appliances they will bring forth exquisite fabrics: garments for personal wear, bedclothes, and the like. When they can afford it they make carpets.

They have, as a rule, luxuriant hair. In some counties one is struck by the purity of the Saxon type, and their faces in early life are often handsome. But one hears that in certain localities they are prone to lose their teeth, and that after the age of thirty-five it is a rare thing to see a woman whose teeth are not partly or wholly wanting. The reason is not apparent. They appear passionately fond of dress, and array themselves in gay colors and in jewelry (pinchbeck), if their worldly es-

Through Cumberland Gap on Horseback

tate justifies the extravagance. Oftener, if young, they have a modest, shy air, as if conscious that their garb is not decorous. Whether married or unmarried, they show much natural diffidence. It is told that in remoter districts of the mountains they are not allowed to sit at the table with the male members of the household, but serve them as in ancient societies. Commonly, in going to church, the men ride and carry the children, while the women walk. Dancing in some regions is hardly known, but in others is a favorite amusement, and in its movements men and women show grace. The mountain preachers oppose it as a sin.

Marriages take place early. They are a fecund race. I asked them time and again to fix upon the average number of children to a family, and they gave as the result seven. In case of parental opposition to wedlock, the lovers run off. There is among the people a low standard of morality in their domestic relations, the delicate privacies of home life having little appreciation where so many persons, without regard to age or sex, are crowded together within very limited quarters.

The dwellings — often mere cabins with a single room — are built of rough-hewn logs, chinked or daubed, though not always. Often there is a puncheon floor and no chamber roof.

Through Cumberland Gap on Horseback

One of these mountaineers, called into court to testify as to the household goods of a defendant neighbor, gave in as the inventory, a string of pumpkins, a skillet without a handle, and "a wild Bill." "A wild Bill" is a bed made by boring auger-holes into a log, driving sticks into these, and overlaying them with hickory bark and sedge-grass—a favorite couch. The low chimneys, made usually of laths daubed, are so low that the saying, inelegant though true, is current, that you may sit by the fire inside and spit out over the top. The cracks in the walls are often large enough to give ingress and egress to child or dog. Even cellars are little known, potatoes sometimes being kept during winter in a hole dug under the hearthstone. More frequently a trap-door is made through the plank flooring in the middle of the room, and in a hole beneath are put potatoes, and, in case of wealth, jellies and preserves. Despite the wretchedness of their habitations and the rigors of mountain climate, they do not suffer with cold, and one may see them out in snow knee-deep clad in low brogans, and nothing heavier than a jeans coat and hunting shirt.

The customary beverage is coffee, bitter and black, not having been roasted but burned. All drink it, from the youngest up. Another beverage is "mountain tea," which is made

Through Cumberland Gap on Horseback

from the sweet-scented golden-rod and from winter-green—the New England checkerberry. These decoctions they mollify with home-made sorghum molasses, which they call " long sweetening," or with sugar, which by contrast is known as "short sweetening."

Of home government there is little or none, boys especially setting aside at will parental authority; but a sort of traditional sense of duty and decorum restrains them by its silent power, and moulds them into respect. Children while quite young are often plump to roundness, but soon grow thin and white and meagre like the parents. There is little desire for knowledge or education. The mountain schools have sometimes less than half a dozen pupils during the few months they are in session. A gentleman who wanted a coal bank opened, engaged for the work a man passing along the road. Some days later he learned that his workman was a school-teacher, who, in consideration of the seventy-five cents a day, had dismissed his academy.

Many, allured by rumors from the West, have migrated thither, but nearly all come back, from love of the mountains, from indisposition to cope with the rush and vigor and enterprise of frontier life. Theirs, they say, is a good lazy man's home.

Through Cumberland Gap on Horseback

Their customs respecting the dead are interesting. When a husband dies his funeral sermon is not preached, but the death of the wife is awaited, and vice versa. Then a preacher is sent for, friend and neighbor called in, and the respect is paid both together. Often two or three preachers are summoned, and each delivers a sermon. More peculiar is the custom of having the services for one person repeated; so that the dead get their funerals preached several times, months and years after their burial. I heard of the pitiful story of two sisters who had their mother's funeral preached once every summer as long as they lived. You may engage the women in mournful conversation respecting the dead, but hardly the men. In strange contrast with this regard for ceremonial observances is their neglect of the graves of their beloved, which they do not seem at all to visit when once closed, or to decorate with those symbols of affection which are the common indications of bereavement.

Nothing that I have ever seen is so lonely, so touching in its neglect and wild, irreparable solitude, as one of these mountain graveyards. On some knoll under a clump of trees, or along some hill-side where dense oak-trees make a mid-day gloom, you walk amid the unknown, undistinguishable dead. Which was father

Through Cumberland Gap on Horseback

and which mother, where are lover and stricken sweetheart, whether this is the dust of laughing babe or crooning grandam, you will never know : no foot-stones, no head-stones; sometimes a few rough rails laid around, as you would make a little pen for swine. In places, however, one sees a picket-fence put up, or a sort of shed built over.

Traditions and folk-lore among them are evanescent, and vary widely in different localities. It appears that in part they are sprung from the early hunters who came into the mountains when game was abundant, sport unfailing, living cheap. Among them now are still-hunters, who know the haunts of bear and deer, needing no dogs. They even now prefer wild meat—even "'possum" and "'coon" and ground-hog—to any other. In Bell County I spent the day in the house of a woman eighty years old, who was a lingering representative of a nearly extinct type. She had never been out of the neighborhood of her birth, knew the mountains like a garden, had whipped men in single-handed encounter, brought down many a deer and wild turkey with her own rifle, and now, infirm, had but to sit in her cabin door and send her trained dogs into the depths of the forests to discover the wished-for game. A fiercer woman I never looked on.

III

OUR course now lay direct towards Cumberland Gap, some twenty miles southward. Our road ran along the bank of the Cumberland River to the ford, the immemorial crossing-place of early travel—and a beautiful spot—thence to Pineville, situated in that narrow opening in Pine Mountain where the river cuts it, and thence through the valley of Yellow Creek to the wonderful pass. The scenery in this region is one succession of densely wooded mountains, blue-tinted air, small cultivated tracts in the fertile valleys, and lovely watercourses.

Along the first part of our route the river slips crystal-clear over its rocky bed, and beneath the lone green pendent branches of the trees that crowd the banks. At the famous ford it was only two or three feet deep at the time of our crossing. This is a historic point. Here was one of the oldest settlements in the country; here the Federal army destroyed the

Through Cumberland Gap on Horseback

houses and fences during the Civil War; and here Zollikoffer came to protect the Kentucky gate that opens into East Tennessee. At Pineville, just beyond, we did not remain long. For some reason not clearly understood by travellers, a dead-line has been drawn through the midst of the town, and not knowing on which side we were entitled to stand, we hastened on to a place where we might occupy neutral ground.

The situation is strikingly picturesque: the mountain looks as if cleft sheer and fallen apart, the peaks on each side rising almost perpendicularly, with massive overhanging crests wooded to the summits, but showing gray rifts of the inexhaustible limestone. The river when lowest is here at an elevation of nine hundred and sixty feet, and the peaks leap to the height of twenty-two hundred. Here in the future will most probably pass a railroad, and be a populous town, for here is the only opening through Pine Mountain from "the brakes" of Sandy to the Tennessee line, and tributary to the watercourses that centre here are some five hundred thousand acres of timber land.

The ride from Pineville to the Gap, fourteen miles southward, is most beautiful. Yellow Creek becomes in local pronunciation "Yaller Crick." One cannot be long in eastern Ken-

Through Cumberland Gap on Horseback

tucky without being struck by the number and character of the names given to the watercourses, which were the natural avenues of migratory travel. Few of the mountains have names. What a history is shut up in these names! Cutshin Creek, where some pioneer, they say, damaged those useful members; but more probably where grows a low greenbrier which cuts the shins and riddles the pantaloons. These pioneers had humor. They named one creek "Troublesome," for reasons apparent to him who goes there; another, "No Worse Creek," on equally good grounds; another, "Defeated Creek"; and a great many, "Lost Creek." In one part of the country it is possible for one to enter "Hell fur Sartain," and get out at "Kingdom Come." Near by are "Upper Devil" and "Lower Devil." One day we went to a mountain meeting which was held in "a school-house and church-house" on "Stinking Creek." One might suppose they would have worshipped in a more fragrant locality; but the stream is very beautiful, and not malodorous. It received its name from its former canebrakes and deer licks, which made game abundant. Great numbers were killed for choice bits of venison and hides. Then there are "Ten-mile Creek" and "Sixteen-mile Creek," meaning to clinch the distance by name; and what is philologically in-

Through Cumberland Gap on Horseback

teresting, one finds numerous "*Trace* Forks," originally "*Trail* Forks."

Bell County and the Yellow Creek Valley serve to illustrate the incalculable mineral and timber resources of eastern Kentucky. Our road at times cut through forests of magnificent timbers — oak (black and white), walnut (black and white), poplar, maple, and chestnut, beech, lynn, gum, dogwood, and elm. Here are some of the finest coal-fields in the world, the one on Clear Creek being fourteen feet thick. Here are pure cannel-coals and coking-coals. At no other point in the Mississippi Valley are iron ores suitable for steel-making purposes so close to fuel so cheap. With an eastern coal-field of 10,000 square miles, with an area equally large covered with a virgin growth of the finest economic timbers, with watercourses feasible and convenient, it cannot be long before eastern Kentucky will be opened up to great industries. Enterprise has already turned hither, and the distinctiveness of the mountaineer race already begins to disappear. The two futures before them are, to be swept out of these mountains by the in-rushing spirit of contending industries, or to be aroused, civilized, and developed.

Long before you come in sight of the great Gap, the idea of it dominates the mind. While

Through Cumberland Gap on Horseback

yet some miles away, it looms up, 1675 feet in elevation, some half a mile across from crest to crest, the pinnacle on the left towering to the height of 2500 feet.

It was late in the afternoon when our tired horses began the long, winding, rocky climb from the valley to the brow of the pass. As we stood in the passway, amid the deepening shadows of the twilight and the solemn repose of the mighty landscape, the Gap seemed to be crowded with two invisible and countless pageants of human life, the one passing in, the other passing out; and the air grew thick with unheard utterances—primeval sounds, undistinguishable and strange, of creatures nameless and never seen by man; the wild rush and whoop of retreating and pursuing tribes; the slow steps of watchful pioneers; the wail of dying children and the songs of homeless women; the muffled tread of routed and broken armies—all the sounds of surprise and delight, victory and defeat, hunger and pain, and weariness and despair, that the human heart can utter. Here passed the first of the white race who led the way into the valley of the Cumberland; here passed that small band of fearless men who gave the Gap its name; here passed the "Long Hunters"; here rushed the armies of the Civil War; here has passed the

Through Cumberland Gap on Horseback

wave of westerly emigration, whose force has spent itself only on the Pacific slopes; and here in the long future must flow backward and forward the wealth of the North and the South.

MOUNTAIN PASSES OF THE CUMBERLAND

I

THE writer has been publishing during the last few years a series of articles on Kentucky. With this article the series will be brought to a close. Hitherto he has written of nature in the Blue-grass Region and of certain aspects of life; but as he comes to take leave of his theme, he finds his attention fixed upon that great mountain wall which lies along the southeastern edge of the State. At various points of this wall are now beginning to be enacted new scenes in the history of Kentucky; and what during a hundred years has been an inaccessible background, is becoming the fore-front of a civilization which will not only change the life of the State within, but advance it to a commanding position in national economic affairs.

But it should not be lost sight of that in writing this article, as in writing all the others, it is with the human problem in Kentucky that he is solely concerned. He will seem to be deal-

Mountain Passes of the Cumberland

ing with commercial activities for their own sake. He will write of coals and ores and timbers, of ovens and tunnels and mines; but if the reader will bear with him to the end, he will learn that these are dealt with only for the sake of looking beyond them at the results which they bring on: town-making in various stages, the massing and distributing of wealth, the movements of population, the dislodgment of isolated customs—on the whole, results that lie in the domain of the human problem in its deepest phases.

Consider for a moment, then, what this great wall is, and what influence it has had over the history of Kentucky and upon the institutions and characteristics of its people.

You may begin at the western frontier of Kentucky on the Mississippi River, about five hundred miles away, and travel steadily eastward across the billowy plateau of the State, going up and up all the time until you come to its base, and above its base it rises to the height of some three thousand feet. For miles before you reach it you discover that it is defended by a zone of almost inaccessible hills with steep slopes, forests difficult to penetrate, and narrow jagged gorges; and further defended by a single sharp wall-like ridge, having an elevation of about twenty-two hundred feet, and lying near-

Mountain Passes of the Cumberland

ly parallel with it, at a distance of about twenty miles. Or, if you should attempt to reach this wall from the south, you would discover that from that side also it is hardly less hostile to approach. Hence it has stood in its virgin wilderness, a vast isolating and isolated barrier, fierce, beautiful, storm-racked, serene; in winter, brown and gray, with its naked woods and rifts of stone, or mantled in white; in summer, green, or of all greens from darkest to palest, and touched with all shades of bloom; in autumn, colored like the sunset clouds; curtained all the year by exquisite health-giving atmospheres, lifting itself all the year towards lovely, changing skies.

Understand the position of this natural fortress-line with regard to the area of Kentucky. That area has somewhat the shape of an enormous flat foot, with a disjointed big toe, a roughly hacked-off ankle, and a missing heel. The sole of this huge foot rests solidly on Tennessee, the Ohio River trickles across the ankle and over the top, the big toe is washed entirely off by the Tennessee River, and the long-missing heel is to be found in Virginia, never having been ceded by that State. Between the Kentucky foot and the Virginia heel is piled up this immense, bony, grisly mass of the Cumberland Mountain, extending

Mountain Passes of the Cumberland

some three hundred miles northeast and south-west.

It was through this heel that Kentucky had to be peopled. The thin, half-starved, weary line of pioneer civilizers had to penetrate it, and climb this obstructing mountain wall, as a line of travelling ants might climb the wall of a castle. In this case only the strongest of the ants—the strongest in body, the strongest in will—succeeded in getting over and establishing their colony in the country far beyond. Luckily there was an enormous depression in the wall, or they might never have scaled it. During about half a century this depression was the difficult, exhausting entrance-point through which the State received the largest part of its people, the furniture of their homes, and the implements of their civilization; so that from the very outset that people represented the most striking instance of a survival of the fittest that may be observed in the founding of any American commonwealth. The feeblest of the ants could not climb the wall; the idlest of them would not. Observe, too, that, once on the other side, it was as hard to get back as it had been to get over. That is, the Cumberland Mountain kept the little ultramontane society isolated. Being isolated, it was kept pure-blooded. Being isolated, it

Mountain Passes of the Cumberland

developed the spirit and virtues engendered by isolation. Hence those traits for which Kentuckians were once, and still think themselves, distinguished—passion for self-government, passion for personal independence, bravery, fortitude, hospitality. On account of this mountain barrier the entire civilization of the State has had a one-sided development. It has become known for pasturage and agriculture, whiskey, hemp, tobacco, and fine stock. On account of it the great streams of colonization flowing from the North towards the South, and flowing from the Atlantic seaboard towards the West, have divided and passed around Kentucky as waters divide and pass around an island, uniting again on the farther side. It has done the like for the highways of commerce, so that the North has become woven to the South and the East woven to the West by a connecting tissue of railroads, dropping Kentucky out as though it had no vital connection, as though it were not a controlling point of connection, for the four sections of the country. Thus keeping out railroads, it has kept out manufactures, kept out commerce, kept out industrial cities. For three-quarters of a century generations of young Kentuckians have had to seek pursuits of this character in other quarters, thus establishing a con-

Mountain Passes of the Cumberland

stant draining away from the State of its resolute, vigorous manhood. Restricting the Kentuckians who have remained to an agricultural type of life, it has brought upon them a reputation for lack of enterprise. More than all this has that great barrier wall done for the history of Kentucky. For, within a hundred years, the only thing to take possession of it, slowly, sluggishly overspreading the region of its foot-hills, its vales and fertile slopes —the only thing to take possession of it and to claim it has been a race of mountaineers, an idle, shiftless, ignorant, lawless population, whose increasing numbers, pauperism, and lawlessness, whose family feuds and clan-like vendettas, have for years been steadily gaining for Kentucky the reputation for having one of the worst backwoods populations on the continent, or, for that matter, in the world.

But for the presence of this wall the history of the State—indeed the history of the United States—would have been profoundly different. Long ago, in virtue of its position, Kentucky would have knit together, instead of holding apart, the North and the South. The campaigns and the results of the Civil War would have been changed; the Civil War might never have taken place. But standing as it has stood, it has left Kentucky, near the close of the first

Mountain Passes of the Cumberland

century of its existence as a State, with a reputation somewhat like the shape of its territory —unsymmetric, mutilated, and with certain parts missing. But now consider this wall of the Cumberland Mountain from another point of view. If you should stand on the crest at any point where it forms the boundary of Kentucky; or south of it, where it extends into Tennessee; or north of it, where it extends into Virginia— if you should stand thus and look northward, you would look out upon a vast area of coal. For many years now it has been known that the coal-measure rocks of eastern Kentucky comprise about a fourth of the area of the State, and are not exceeded in value by those of any other State. It has been known that this buried solar force exceeds that of Great Britain. Later it has become known that the Kentucky portion of the great Appalachian coal-field contains the largest area of rich cannel-coals yet discovered, these having been traced in sixteen counties, and some of them excelling by test the famous cannel-coal of Great Britain; later it has become known that here is to be found the largest area of coking-coal yet discovered, the main coal— discovered a few years ago, and named the "Elkhorn"—having been traced over sixteen

Mountain Passes of the Cumberland

hundred square miles, and equalling American standard coke in excellence.

Further, looking northward, you look out upon a region of iron ores, the deposits in Kentucky ranking sixth in variety and extent among those to be found in all other States, and being better disposed for working than any except those of Virginia, Tennessee, and Alabama. For a hundred years now, it should be remembered in this connection, iron has been smelted in Kentucky, and been an important article of commerce. As early as 1823 it was made at Cumberland Gap, and shipped by river to markets as remote as New Orleans and St. Louis. At an early date, also, it was made in a small charcoal forge at Big Creek Gap, and was hauled in wagons into central Kentucky, where it found a ready market for such purposes as plough-shares and wagon tires.

Further, looking northward, you have extending far and wide before you the finest primeval region of hard-woods in America.

Suppose, now, that you turn and look from this same crest of the Cumberland Mountain southward, or towards the Atlantic seaboard. In that direction there lie some two hundred and fifty thousand square miles of country which is practically coalless; but practically coalless, it is incalculably rich in iron ores

Mountain Passes of the Cumberland

for the manufacture of iron and steel. You look out upon the new industrial empire of the United States, with vast and ever-growing needs of manufactures, fuel, and railroads. That is, for a hundred miles you stand on the dividing line of two distinct geological formations : to the north, the Appalachian coal-fields; to the south, mountains of iron ores ; rearing itself between these, this immense barrier wall, which creates an unapproachable wilderness not only in southeastern Kentucky, but in East Tennessee, western Virginia, and western North Carolina—the largest extent of country in the United States remaining undeveloped.

But the time had to come when this wilderness would be approached on all sides, attacked, penetrated to the heart. Such wealth of resources could not be let alone or remain unused. As respects the development of the region, the industrial problem may be said to have taken two forms—the one, the development of the coal and iron on opposite sides of the mountains, the manufacture of coke and iron and steel, the establishment of wood-working industries, and the delivery of all products to the markets of the land ; second, the bringing together of the coals on the north side and the ores throughout the south. In this way, then, the Cumberland Mountain no longer offered a barrier

Mountain Passes of the Cumberland

merely to the civilization of Kentucky, but to the solution of the greatest economic problem of the age—the cheapest manufacture of iron and steel. But before the pressure of this need the mountain had to give way and surrender its treasures. At any cost of money and labor, the time had to come when it would pay to bring these coals and ores together. But how was this to be done? The answer was simple: it must be done by means of natural water gaps and by tunnels through the mountain. It is the object of this paper to call attention to the way in which the new civilization of the South is expected to work at four mountain passes, and to point out some of the results which are to follow.

II

ON the Kentucky side of the mighty wall of the Cumberland Mountain, and nearly parallel with it, is the sharp single wall of Pine Mountain, the westernmost ridge of the Alleghany system. For about a hundred miles these two gnarled and ancient monsters lie crouched side by side, guarding between them their hidden stronghold of treasure—an immense valley of timbers and irons and coals. Near the middle point of this inner wall there occurs a geological fault. The mountain falls apart as though cut in twain by some heavy downward stroke, showing on the faces of the fissure precipitous sides wooded to the crests. There is thus formed the celebrated and magnificent pass through which the Cumberland River—one of the most beautiful in the land—slips silently out of its mountain valley, and passes on to the hills and the plateaus of Kentucky. In the gap there is a space for the bed of this river, and on each side of

Mountain Passes of the Cumberland

the river space for a roadway and nothing more.

Note the commanding situation of this inner pass. Travel east along Pine Mountain or travel west, and you find no other water gap within a hundred miles. Through this that thin, toiling line of pioneer civilizers made its way, having scaled the great outer Cumberland wall some fifteen miles southward. But for this single geological fault, by which a water gap of the inner mountain was placed opposite a depression in the outer mountain, thus creating a continuous passway through both, the colonization of Kentucky, difficult enough even with this advantage, would have been indefinitely delayed, or from this side wholly impossible. Through this inner portal was traced in time the regular path of the pioneers, afterwards known as the Wilderness Road. On account of the travel over this road and the controlling nature of the site, there was long ago formed on the spot a little backwoods settlement, calling itself Pineville. It consisted of a single straggling line of cabins and shanties of logs on each side of a roadway, this road being the path of the pioneers. In the course of time it was made the county-seat. Being the county-seat, the way-side village, catching every traveller on foot or on horse or in wagons, began

Mountain Passes of the Cumberland

some years ago to make itself still better known as the scene of mountain feuds. The name of the town when uttered anywhere in Kentucky suggested but one thing—a blot on the civilization of the State, a mountain fastness where the human problem seems most intractable. A few such places have done more to foster the unfortunate impression which Kentucky has made upon the outside world than all the towns of the blue-grass country put together.

Five summers ago, in 1885, in order to prepare an article for HARPER'S MAGAZINE on the mountain folk of the Cumberland region, I made my way towards this mountain town, now riding on a buck-board, now on a horse whose back was like a board that was too stiff to buck. The road I travelled was that great highway between Kentucky and the South, which at various times within a hundred years has been known as the Wilderness Road, or the Cumberland Road, or the National Turnpike, or the "Kaintuck Hog Road," as it was called by the mountaineers. It is impossible to come upon this road without pausing, or to write of it without a tribute. It led from Baltimore over the mountains of Virginia through the great wilderness by Cumberland Gap. All roads below Philadelphia converged at this gap, just as the buffalo and Indian trails had

Mountain Passes of the Cumberland

earlier converged, and just as many railroads are converging now. The improvement of this road became in time the pet scheme of the State governments of Virginia and Kentucky. Before the war millions of head of stock—horses, hogs, cattle, mules—were driven over it to the southern markets; and thousands of vehicles, with families and servants and trunks, have somehow passed over it, coming northward into Kentucky, or going southward on pleasure excursions. During the war vast commissary stores passed back and forth, following the movement of armies. But despite all this—despite all that has been done to civilize it since Boone traced its course in 1790, this honored historic thoroughfare remains to-day as it was in the beginning, with all its sloughs and sands, its mud and holes, and jutting ledges of rock and loose bowlders, and twists and turns, and general total depravity.

It is not surprising that when the original Kentuckians were settled on the blue-grass plateau they sternly set about the making of good roads, and to this day remain the best road-builders in America. One such road was enough. They are said to have been notorious for profanity, those who came into Kentucky from this side. Naturally. Many were infidels—there are roads that make a man lose faith.

Mountain Passes of the Cumberland

It is known that the more pious companies of them, as they travelled along, would now and then give up in despair, sit down, raise a hymn, and have prayers before they could go farther. Perhaps one of the provocations to homicide among the mountain people should be reckoned this road. I have seen two of the mildest of men, after riding over it for a few hours, lose their temper and begin to fight—fight their horses, fight the flies, fight the cobwebs on their noses, fight anything.

Over this road, then, and towards this town, one day, five summers ago, I was picking my course, but not without pale human apprehensions. At that time one did not visit Pineville for nothing. When I reached it I found it tense with repressed excitement. Only a few days previous there had been a murderous affray in the streets; the inhabitants had taken sides; a dead-line had been drawn through the town, so that those living on either side crossed to the other at the risk of their lives; and there was blue murder in the air. I was a stranger; I was innocent; I was peaceful. But I was told that to be a stranger and innocent and peaceful did no good. Stopping to eat, I fain would have avoided, only it seemed best not to be murdered for refusing. All that I now remember of the dinner was a corn-bread that

Mountain Passes of the Cumberland

would have made a fine building stone, being of an attractive bluish tint, hardening rapidly upon exposure to the atmosphere, and being susceptible of a high polish. A block of this, freshly quarried, I took, and then was up and away. But not quickly, for having exchanged my horse for another, I found that the latter moved off as though at every step expecting to cross the dead-line, and so perish. The impression of the place was one never to be forgotten, with its squalid hovels, its ragged armed men collected suspiciously in little groups, with angry, distrustful faces, or peering out from behind the ambush of a window.

A few weeks ago I went again to Pineville, this time by means of one of the most extensive and powerful railroad systems of the South. At the station a 'bus was waiting to take passengers to the hotel. The station was on one side of the river, the hotel on the other. We were driven across a new iron bridge, this being but one of four now spanning the river formerly crossed at a single ford. At the hotel we were received by a porter of metropolitan urbanity and self-esteem. Entering the hotel, I found it lighted by gas, and full of guests from different parts of the United States. In the lobby there was a suppressed murmur of refined voices coming from groups engaged in

Mountain Passes of the Cumberland

serious talk. As by-and-by I sat in a spacious dining-room, looking over a freshly printed bill of fare, some one in the parlors opposite was playing on the piano airs from "Tannhäuser" and "Billee Taylor." The dining-room was animated by a throng of brisk, tidy, white young waiting-girls, some of whom were far too pretty to look at except from behind a thick napkin; and presently, to close this experience of the new Pineville, there came along such inconceivable flannel-cakes and molasses that, forgetting industrial and social problems, I gave myself up to the enjoyment of a problem personal and gastric; and ere long, having spread myself between snowy sheets, I melted away, as the butter between the cakes, into warm slumber, having first poured over myself a syrup of thanksgiving.

The next morning I looked out of my window upon a long pleasant valley, mountain-sheltered, and crossed by the winding Cumberland; here and there cottages of a smart modern air already built or building; in another direction, business blocks of brick and stone, graded streets and avenues and macadamized roads; and elsewhere, saw and planing mills, coke ovens, and other evidences of commercial development. Through the open door of a church I saw a Catholic congregation already on its

Mountain Passes of the Cumberland

knees, and the worshippers of various Protestant denominations were looking towards their own temples. The old Pineville, happily situated farther down the river, at the very opening of the pass, was rapidly going to ruins. The passion for homicide had changed into a passion for land speculation. The very man on whose account at my former visit the old Pineville had been divided into two deadly factions, whose name throughout all the region once stood for mediæval violence, had become a real-estate agent. I was introduced to him.

"Sir," said I, "I don't feel so *very* much afraid of you."

"Sir," said he, "I don't like to run myself."

Such, briefly, is the impression made by the new Pineville—a new people there, new industries, new moral atmosphere, new civilization.

The explanation of this change is not far to seek. By virtue of its commanding position as the only inner gateway to the North, this pass was the central point of distribution for southeastern Kentucky. Flowing into the Cumberland, on the north side of the mountain, is Clear Creek, and on the south side is Strait Creek, the two principal streams of this region, and supplying water-power and drainage. Tributary to these streams are, say, half

Mountain Passes of the Cumberland

a million acres of noble timber land; in the mountains around, the best coals, coking and domestic; elsewhere, iron ores, pure brown, hematite, and carbonates; inexhaustible quantities of limestone, blue-gray sandstone, brick clays; gushing from the mountains, abundant streams of healthful freestone water; on the northern hill-sides, a deep loam suitable for grass and gardens and fruits. Add to this that through this water-gap, following the path of the Wilderness Road, as the Wilderness Road had followed the path of the Indian and the buffalo—through this water-gap would have to pass all railroads that should connect the North and South by means of that historic and ancient highway of traffic and travel.

On the basis of these facts, three summers ago a few lawyers in Louisville bought 300 acres of land near the riotous old town of Pineville, and in the same summer was organized the Pine Mountain Iron and Coal Company, which now, however, owns about twenty thousand acres, with a capital stock of $2,000,000. It should be noted that Southern men and native capital began this enterprise, and that although other stockholders are from Chicago and New England, most of the capital remains in the State. Development has been rapidly carried forward, and over five hundred thou-

Mountain Passes of the Cumberland

sand dollars' worth of lots have been sold the present year. It is pleasant to dwell upon the future that is promised for this place; pleasant to hear that over six hundred acres in this pleasant valley are to be platted; that there are to be iron-furnaces and electric lights, concrete sidewalks and a street railway, more bridges, brick-yards, and a high-school; and that the seventy-five coke ovens now in blast are to be increased to a thousand. Let it be put down to the credit of this vigorous little mountain town that it is the first place in that region to put Kentucky coke upon the market, and create a wide demand for it in remote quarters—Cincinnati alone offering to take the daily output of five hundred ovens.

Thus the industrial and human problems are beginning to solve themselves side by side in the backwoods of Kentucky. You begin with coke and end with Christianity. It is the boast of Pineville that as soon as it begins to make its own iron it can build its houses without calling on the outside world for an ounce of material.

III

MIDDLESBOROUGH! For a good many years in England and throughout the world the name has stood associated with wealth and commercial greatness —the idea of a powerful city near the mouth of the Tees, in the North Riding of Yorkshire, which has become the principal seat of the English iron trade. It is, therefore, curious to remember that near the beginning of the century there stood on the site of this powerful city four farm-houses and a ruined shrine of St. Hilda; that it took thirty years to bring the population up to the number of one hundred and fifty-four souls; that the discovery of iron-stone, as it seems to be called on that side, gave it a boom, as it is called on this; so that ten years ago it had some sixty thousand people, its hundred and thirty blast-furnaces, besides other industries, and an annual output in pig-iron of nearly two million tons.

But there is now an English Middlesborough

Mountain Passes of the Cumberland

in America, which is already giving to the name another significance in the stock market of London and among the financial journals of the realm; and if the idea of its founders is ever realized, if its present rate of development goes on, it will in time represent as much wealth in gold and iron as the older city.

In the mere idea of the American or Kentucky Middlesborough—for while it seems to be meant for America, it is to be found in Kentucky—there is something to arrest attention on the score of originality. That the attention of wealthy commoners, bankers, scientists, and iron-masters of Great Britain—some of them men long engaged in copper, tin, and gold mines in the remotest quarters of the globe—that the attention of such men should be focused on a certain spot in the backwoods of Kentucky; that they should repeatedly send over experts to report on the combination of mineral and timber wealth; that on the basis of such reports they should form themselves into a company called "The American Association, Limited," and purchase 60,000 acres of land lying on each side of the Cumberland Mountain and around the meeting-point of the States of Virginia, Tennessee, and Kentucky; that an allied association, called "The Middlesborough Town Company," should place

Mountain Passes of the Cumberland

here the site of a city, with the idea of making it the principal seat of the iron and steel manufacture of the United States; that they should go to work to create this city outright by pouring in capital for every needed purpose; that they should remove gigantic obstacles in order to connect it with the national highways of commerce; that they should thus expend some twenty million dollars, and let it be known that all millions further wanted were forthcoming—in the idea of this there is enough to make one pause.

As one cannot ponder the idea of the enterprise without being impressed with its largeness, so one cannot visit the place without being struck by the energy with which the plan is being wrought at. " It is not sufficient to know that this property possesses coal and iron of good quality and in considerable quantities, and that the deposits are situated close together, but that they exist in such circumstances as will give us considerable advantages over any competitors that either now exist or whose existence can in any way be foreseen in the near future." Such were the instructions of these English capitalists to their agent in America. It was characteristic of their race and of that method of business by which they have become the masters of commerce the

Mountain Passes of the Cumberland

world over. In it is the germ of their idea—to establish a city for the manufacture of iron and steel which, by its wealth of resources, advantages of situation, and complete development, should place competition at a disadvantage, and thus make it impossible.

It yet remains to be seen whether this can be done. Perhaps even the hope of it came from an inadequate knowledge of how vast a region they had entered, and how incalculable its wealth. Perhaps it was too much to expect that any one city, however situated, however connected, however developed, should be able to absorb or even to control the development of that region and the distribution of its resources to all points of the land. It suggests the idea of a single woodpecker's hoping to carry off the cherries from a tree which a noble company of cats and jays and other birds were watching; or of a family of squirrels who should take up their abode in a certain hole with the idea of eating all the walnuts in a forest. But, however this may turn out, these Englishmen, having once set before themselves their aim, have never swerved from trying to attain it; and they are at work developing their city with the hope that it will bring as great a change in the steel market of the United States as a few years ago was

Mountain Passes of the Cumberland

made in the iron market by the manufacture of Southern iron.

If you take up in detail the working out of their plan of development, it is the same—no stint, no drawing back or swerving aside, no abatement of the greatest intentions. They must have a site for their city—they choose for this site what with entire truthfulness may be called one of the most strategic mountain passes in American history. They must have a name—they choose that of the principal seat of the English iron trade. They must have a plant for the manufacture of steel by the basic process—they promise it shall be the largest in the United States. They want a tannery—it shall be the biggest in the world. A creek has to be straightened to improve drainage—they spend on it a hundred thousand dollars. They will have their mineral resources known—they order a car to be built, stock it with an exposition of their minerals, place it in charge of technical experts, and set it going over the country. They take a notion to establish a casino, sanitarium, and hotel—it must cost over seven hundred thousand dollars. The mountain is in their way—that mighty wall of the Cumberland Mountain which has been in the way of the whole United States for over a hundred years—they remove this moun-

Mountain Passes of the Cumberland

tain; that is, they dig through it a great union tunnel, 3750 feet long, beginning in Kentucky, running under a corner of Virginia, and coming out in Tennessee. Had they done nothing but this, they would have done enough to entitle them to the gratitude of the nation, for it is an event of national importance. It brings the South and the Atlantic seaboard in connection with the Ohio Valley and the Lakes; it does more to make the North and the South one than any other single thing that has happened since the close of the Civil War.

On the same trip that took me to Pineville five summers ago, I rode from that place southward towards the wall of Cumberland Mountain. I wished to climb this wall at that vast depression in it known as Cumberland Gap. It was a tranquil afternoon as I took my course over the ancient Wilderness Road through the valley of the Yellow Creek. Many a time since the memory of that ride has come back to me —the forests of magnificent timbers, open spaces of cleared land showing the amphitheatre of hills in the purple distance, the winding of a shadowy green-banked stream, the tranquil loneliness, the purity of primeval solitude. The flitting of a bird between one and the azure sky overhead was company, a wild flower bending over the water's edge was friendship. Noth-

FORD ON THE CUMBERLAND

Mountain Passes of the Cumberland

ing broke rudely in upon the spirit of the scene but here and there a way-side log-cabin, with its hopeless squalor, hopeless human inmates. If imagination sought relief from loneliness, it found it only in conjuring from the dust of the road that innumerable caravan of life from barbarism to civilization, from the savage to the soldier, that has passed hither and thither, leaving the wealth of nature unravished, its solitude unbroken.

In the hush of the evening and amid the silence of eternity, I drew the rein of my tired horse on the site of the present town. Before me in the mere distance, and outlined against the glory of the sky, there towered at last the mighty mountain wall, showing the vast depression of the gap—the portal to the greatness of the commonwealth. Stretching away in every direction was a wide plain, broken here and there by wooded knolls, and uniting itself with graceful curves to the gentle slopes of the surrounding mountains. The ineffable beauty, the vast repose, the overawing majesty of the historic portal, the memories, the shadows—they are never to be forgotten.

A few weeks ago I reached the same spot as the sun was rising, having come thither from Pineville by rail. As I stepped from the train I saw that the shadowy valley of my remem-

Mountain Passes of the Cumberland

brance had been incredibly transformed. Some idea of the plan of the new town may be understood from the fact that Cumberland Avenue and Peterborough Avenue, intersecting each other near the central point of it, are, when completed, to be severally three and a half or four and a half miles long. There are twenty avenues and thirty streets in all, ranging from a hundred feet to sixty feet wide. So long and broad and level are the thoroughfares that the plan, as projected, suggests comparison with Louisville. The valley site itself contains some six thousand available acres.

It should be understood that the company owns property on the Tennessee side of the gap, and that at the foot of the valley, where a magnificent spring gushes out, with various other mineral springs near by—chalybeate and sulphur—it is proposed to establish a hotel, sanitarium, and casino which shall equal in sumptuousness the most noted European spas.

As I stood one day in this valley, which has already begun to put on the air of civilization, with its hotel and railway station and mills and pretty homesteads, I saw a sight which seemed to me a complete epitome of the past and present tendencies there at work—a summing up of the past and a prophecy of the future. Creeping slowly past the station—so slowly that one

Mountain Passes of the Cumberland

knows not what to compare it to unless it be the minute-hand on the dial of a clock—creeping slowly along the Wilderness Road towards the ascent of Cumberland Gap, there came a mountain wagon, faded and old, with its dirty ragged canvas hanging motionless, and drawn by a yoke of mountain oxen which seemed to be moving in their sleep. On the seat in front, with a faded shovel-hat capping his mass of coarse tangled hair, and wearing but two other garments—a faded shirt and faded breeches—sat a faded, pinched, and meagre mountain boy. The rope with which he drove his yoke had dropped between his clasped knees. He had forgotten it; there was no need to remember it. His starved white face was kindled into an expression of passionate hunger and excitement. In one dirty claw-like hand he grasped a small paper bag, into the open mouth of which he had thrust the other hand, as a miser might thrust his into a bag of gold. He had just bought, with a few cents, some sweetmeat of civilization which he was about for the first time to taste. I sat and watched him move away and begin the ascent to the pass. Slowly, slowly, winding now this way and now that across the face of the mountain, now hidden, now in sight, they went—sleeping oxen, crawling wagon, starved mountain child. At length, as they

Mountain Passes of the Cumberland

were about disappearing through the gap, they passed behind a column of the white steam from a saw-mill that was puffing a short distance in front of me; and, hidden in that steam, they disappeared. It was the last of the mountaineers passing away before the breath of civilization.

IV

SUPPOSE now that you stand on the south side of the great wall of the Cumberland Mountain at Cumberland Gap. You have come through the splendid tunnel beneath, or you have crawled over the summit in the ancient way; but you stand at the base on the Tennessee side in the celebrated Powell's River Valley.

Turn to the left and follow up this valley, keeping the mountain on your left. You are not the first to take this course: the line of human ants used to creep down it in order to climb over the wall at the gap. Mark how inaccessible this wall is at every other point. Mark, also, that as you go two little black parallel iron threads follow you—a railroad, one of the greatest systems of the South. All along the mountain slope overhanging the railroad, iron ore; beyond the mountain crest, timber and coals. Observe, likewise, the features of the land: water abundant, clear, and

Mountain Passes of the Cumberland

cold; fields heavy with corn and oats; an ever-changing panorama of beautiful pictures. The farther you go the more rich and prosperous the land, the kinder the soil to grains and gardens and orchards; bearing its burden of timbers — walnut, chestnut, oak, and mighty beeches; lifting to the eye in the near distance cultivated hill-sides and fat meadows; stretching away into green and shadowy valley glades; tuneful with swift, crystal streams—a land of lovely views.

Remember well this valley, lying along the base of the mountain wall. It has long been known as the granary of southwest Virginia and east Tennessee; but in time, in the development of civilization throughout the Appalachian region, it is expected to become the seat of a dense pastoral population, supplying the dense industrial population of new mining and manufacturing towns with milk, butter, eggs, and fruit and vegetables. But for the contiguity of such agricultural districts to the centres of ores and coals, it would perhaps be impossible to establish in these remote spots the cities necessary to develop and transport their wealth.

Follow this valley up for a distance of sixty miles from Cumberland Gap and there pause, for you come to the head of the valley, and

Mountain Passes of the Cumberland

you have reached another pass in the mountain wall. You have passed out of Tennessee into Virginia, a short distance from the Kentucky border, and the mountain wall is no longer called the Cumberland: twenty miles southwest of where you now are that mountain divided, sending forth this southern prong, called Stone Mountain, and sending the rest of itself between the State line of Kentucky and Virginia, under the name of the Big Black Mountain. Understand, also, the general bearings of the spot at which you have arrived. It is in that same Alleghany system of mountains — the richest metalliferous region in the world — the northern section of which long ago made Pittsburgh; the southern section of which has since created Birmingham; and the middle section of which, where you now are, is claimed by expert testimony, covering a long period of years and coming from different and wholly uninterested authorities, to be the richest of the three.

This mountain pass not being in Kentucky, it might be asked why in a series of articles on Kentucky it should deserve a place. The answer is plain: not because a Kentuckian selected it as the site of a hoped-for city, or because Kentuckians have largely developed it, or because Kentuckians largely own it, and

Mountain Passes of the Cumberland

have stamped upon it a certain excellent social tone; but for the reason that if the idea of its development is carried out, it will gather towards itself a vast net-work of railways from eastern Kentucky, the Atlantic seaboard, the South, and the Ohio and Mississippi valleys, which will profoundly affect the inner life of Kentucky, and change its relations to different parts of the Union.

Big Stone Gap! It does not sound very big. What is it? At a certain point of this continuation of Cumberland Mountain, called Stone Mountain, the main fork of Powell's River has in the course of ages worn itself a way down to a practical railroad pass at water-level, thus opening connection between the coking coal on the north and the iron ores on the south of the mountain. No pass that I have ever seen —except those made by the Doe River in the Cranberry region of North Carolina — has its wild, enrapturing loveliness; towering above on each side are the mountain walls, ancient and gray and rudely disordered; at every coign of vantage in these, grasping their precipitous buttresses, as the claw of a great eagle might grasp the uttermost brow of a cliff, enormous trees above trees, and amid the trees a green lace-work of undergrowth. Below, in a narrow, winding channel piled high with

Mountain Passes of the Cumberland

bowlders, with jutting rocks and sluice-like fissures — below and against these the river hurls itself, foaming, roaring, whirling, a long cascade of white or lucent water. This is Big Stone Gap, and the valley into which the river pours its full strong current is the site of the town. A lofty valley it is, having an elevation of 1600 feet above the sea, with mountains girdling it that rise to the height of 4000—a valley the surface of which gently rolls and slopes towards these encircling bases with constant relief to the eye, and spacious enough, with those opening into it, to hold a city of the population of New York.

This mountain pass, lying in the heart of this reserved wilderness of timbers, coals, and ores, has always had its slender thread of local history. It was from a time immemorial a buffalo and Indian trail, leading to the head-waters of the Cumberland and Kentucky rivers; during the Civil War it played its part in certain local military exploits and personal adventures of a quixotian flavor; and of old the rich farmers of Lee County used to drive their cattle through it to fatten on the pea-vine and blue-grass growing thick on the neighboring mountain tops. But in the last twenty-five years — that quarter of the century which has developed in the United States an ever-growing need of iron and

Mountain Passes of the Cumberland

steel, of hard-woods, and of all varieties of coal; a period which has seen one after another of the reserve timber regions of the country thinned and exhausted—during the past twenty-five years attention has been turned more and more towards the forests and the coal-fields in the region occupied by the south Alleghany Mountain system.

It was not enough to know that at Big Stone Gap there is a water-gap admitting the passage of a railway on each side at water-level, and connecting contiguous workable coals with ores; not enough repeatedly to test the abundance, variety, and purity of both of these; not enough to know that a short distance off a single vertical section of coal-measure rocks has a thickness above drainage level of 2500 feet, the thickest in the entire Appalachian coal-field from Pennsylvania to Alabama; not enough that from this point, by available railroad to the Bessemer steel ores in the Cranberry district of North Carolina, it is the shortest distance in the known world separating such coke and such ores; not enough that there are here superabundant limestone and water, the south fork of Powell's River winding about the valley, a full, bold current, and a few miles from the town the head-waters of this same river having a fall of 700 feet; not enough that near

Mountain Passes of the Cumberland

by is a rich agricultural region to supply needed markets, and that the valley itself has a natural drainage, delightful climate, and ideal beauty—all this was not enough. It had to be known that the great water-gap through the mountain at this point, by virtue of its position and by virtue of its relation to other passes and valleys leading to it, necessitated, sooner or later, a concentration here of railroad lines for the gathering, the development, and the distribution of its resources.

From every imaginable point of view a place like this is subject to unsparing test before it is finally fixed upon as a town site and enters upon a process of development. Nothing would better illustrate the tremendous power with which the new South, hand in hand with a new North, works with brains and capital and science. A few years ago this place was seventy miles from the nearest railroad. That road has since been built to it from the south; a second is approaching it from a distance of a hundred and twenty miles on the west; a third from the east; and when the last two come together this point will be on a great east and west trunk line, connecting the Ohio and Mississippi valleys with the Atlantic seaboard. Moreover, the Legislature of Kentucky has just passed an act incorporating the Inter-State

Mountain Passes of the Cumberland

Tunnel Railroad Company, and empowering it to build an inter-State double-track highway from the head-waters of the Cumberland and Kentucky rivers to Big Stone Gap, tunnelling both the Black and Cumberland Mountains, and affording a passway north and south for the several railways of eastern Kentucky already heading towards this point. The plan embraces two double-track toll tunnels, with double-track approaches between and on each side of the tunnel, to be owned and controlled by a stock company which shall allow all railroads to pass on the payment of toll. If this enterprise, involving the cost of over two million dollars, is carried out, the railroad problem at Big Stone Gap, and with it the problem of developing the mineral wealth of southwest Virginia and southeast Kentucky, would seem to be practically solved.

That so many railroads should be approaching this point from so many different directions seems to lift it at once to a position of extraordinary importance.

But it is only a few months since the nearest one reached there; and, since little could be done towards development otherwise, at Big Stone Gap one sees the process of town-making at an earlier stage than at Middlesborough. Still, there are under construction water-works,

Mountain Passes of the Cumberland

from the pure mountain river, at an elevation of 400 feet, six miles from town, that will supply daily 2,500,000 gallons of water; two iron-furnaces of a hundred tons daily capacity; an electric-light plant, starting with fifty street arc-lights, and 750 incandescent burners for residences, and a colossal hotel of 300 rooms. These may be taken as evidences of the vast scale on which development is to be carried forward, to say nothing of a steam street railway, belt line, lumber and brick and finishing plants, union depot, and a coke plant modelled after that at Connellsville. And on the whole it may be said that already over a million dollars' worth of real estate has been sold, and that eight land, coal, and iron development companies have centred here the development of properties aggregating millions in value.

It is a peculiarity of these industrial towns thus being founded in one of the most beautiful mountain regions of the land that they shall not merely be industrial towns. They aim at becoming cities or homes for the best of people; fresh centres to which shall be brought the newest elements of civilization from the North and South; retreats for jaded pleasure-seekers; asylums for invalids. And therefore they are laid out for amenities and beauty as well as industry—with an eye to using the ex-

Mountain Passes of the Cumberland

quisite mountain flora and park-like forests, the natural boulevards along their watercourses, and the natural roadways to vistas of enchanting mountain scenery. What is to be done at Middlesborough will not be forgotten. At Big Stone Gap, in furtherance of this idea, there has been formed a Mountain Park Association, which has bought some three thousand acres of summit land a few miles from the town, with the idea of making it a game preserve and shooting park, adorned with a rambling club-house in the Swiss style of architecture. In this preserve is High Knob, perhaps the highest mountain in the Alleghany range, being over four thousand feet above sea-level, the broad summit of which is carpeted with blue-grass and white clover in the midst of magnificent forest growth.

V

SUPPOSE once more that you stand outside the Cumberland or Stone Mountain at the gap. Now turn and follow down the beautiful Powell's Valley, retracing your course to Cumberland Gap. Pass this, continuing down the same valley, and keeping on your right the same parallel mountain wall. Mark once more how inaccessible it is at every point. Mark once more the rich land and prosperous tillage. Having gone about thirty miles beyond Cumberland Gap, pause again. You have come to another pass—another remarkable gateway. You have travelled out of Kentucky into Tennessee, and the Cumberland Mountain has changed its name and become Walden's Mountain, distant some fifteen miles from the Kentucky State line.

It is necessary once more to define topographical bearings. Running northeast and southwest is this Cumberland Mountain, having an elevation of from twenty-five hundred

Mountain Passes of the Cumberland

to three thousand feet. Almost parallel with it, from ten to twenty miles away, and having an elevation of about two thousand feet, lies Pine Mountain, in Kentucky. In the outer or Cumberland Mountain it has now been seen that there are three remarkable gaps: Big Stone Gap on the east, where Powell's River cuts through Stone Mountain; Cumberland Gap intermediate, which is not a water-gap, but a depression in the mountain; and Big Creek Gap in the west, where Big Creek cuts through Walden's Mountain — the last being about forty miles distant from the second, about ninety from the first. Now observe that in Pine Mountain there are three water-gaps having a striking relation to the gaps in the Cumberland—that is, behind Cumberland Gap is the pass at Pineville; behind Big Stone Gap and beyond it at the end of the mountain are the Breaks of Sandy; and behind Big Creek Gap are the Narrows, a natural water-gap connecting Tennessee with Kentucky.

But it has been seen that the English have had to tunnel Cumberland Mountain at Middlesborough in order to open the valley between Pine and Cumberland mountains to railroad connections with the south. It has also been seen that at Big Stone Gap it has been found necessary to plan for a vast tunnel under Big

Mountain Passes of the Cumberland

Black Mountain, and also under Pine Mountain, in order to establish north and south connections for railroads, and control the development of southeast Kentucky and southwest Virginia. But now mark the advantage of the situation at Big Creek Gap: a water-gap at railroad level giving entrance from the south, and seventeen miles distant a corresponding water-gap at railroad level giving exit from the south and entrance from the north. There is thus afforded a double natural gateway at this point, and at this point alone—an inestimable advantage. Here, then, is discovered a third district centre in Cumberland Mountain where the new industrial civilization of the South is expected to work. All the general conditions elsewhere stated are here found present—timbers, coals, and ores, limestone, granite, water, scenery, climate, flora; the beauty is the same, the wealth not less.

With a view to development, a company has bought up and owns in fee 20,000 acres of coal lands and some seven thousand of iron ore in the valley and along the foothills on the southern slope of the mountain. They have selected and platted as a town site over sixteen hundred acres of beautiful valley land, lying on both sides of Big Creek where it cuts through the mountain, 1200

Mountain Passes of the Cumberland

feet above the sea-level. But here again one comes upon the process of town-making at a still earlier stage of development. That is, the town exists only on paper, and improvement has not yet begun. Taken now, it is in the stage that Middlesborough, or Big Stone Gap, was once in. So that it should not be thought any the less real because it is rudimentary or embryonic. A glance at the wealth tributary to this point will soon dispel doubt that here in the future, as at the other strategic mountain passes of the Cumberland, is to be established an important town.

Only consider that the entire 20,000 acres owned by the Big Creek Gap Company are underlain by coal, and that the high mountains between the Pine and Cumberland contain vertical sections of greater thickness of coal-measure rocks than are to be found anywhere else in the vast Appalachian field; that Walnut Mountain, on the land of the company—the western continuation of the Black Mountain and the Log Mountain of Kentucky—is 3300 feet above sea, and has 2000 feet of coal-measures above drainage; and that already there has been developed the existence of six coals of workable thickness above drainage level, five of them underlying the entire 20,000

Mountain Passes of the Cumberland

acres, except where small portions have been cut away by the streams.

The lowest coal above drainage—the Sharpe—presents an outcrop about twenty feet above the bed of the stream, and underlies the entire purchase. It has long been celebrated for domestic use in the locality. An entry driven in about sixty feet shows a twelve-inch cannel-coal with a five-inch soft shale, burning with a brilliant flame, and much used in Powell's Valley; also a bituminous coal of forty-three-inch thickness, having a firm roof, cheaply minable, and yielding a coke of over 93 per cent. pure carbon.

The next coal above is a cannel-coal having an outcrop on the Middle Fork of Big Creek of thirty-six inches, and on the north slope of the mountains, six miles off, of thirty-eight inches, showing a persistent bed throughout.

Above this is the Douglass coal, an entry of forty feet into which shows a thickness of fifty inches, with a good roof, and on the northern slope of the mountains, at Cumberland River, a thickness of sixty inches. This is a gas coal of great excellence, yielding also a coke, good, but high in sulphur. Above the Douglass is an unexplored section of great thickness, showing coal stains and coals exposed, but undeveloped.

Mountain Passes of the Cumberland

The uppermost coal discovered, and the highest opened in Tennessee—the Walnut Mountain coal—is a coking variety of superior quality, fifty-eight inches thick, and, though lying near the top of the mountain, protected by a sandstone roof. It is minable at a low cost, admirable for gas, and is here found underlying some two thousand acres.

As to the wealth of iron ores, it has been said that the company owns about seven thousand acres in the valley and along the southern slopes of Cumberland Mountain. There is a continuous outcrop of the soft red fossiliferous, or Clinton, iron ore, ten miles long, nowhere at various outcrops less than sixty inches thick, of exceptional richness and purity, well located for cheap mining, and adjacent to the coal-beds. Indeed, where it crosses Big Creek at the gap, it is only a mile from the coking coal. Lying from one to two hundred feet above the drainage level of the valley, where a railroad is to be constructed, and parallel to this road at a distance of a few hundred feet, this ore can be put on cars and delivered to the furnaces of Big Creek Gap at an estimated cost of a dollar a ton. Of red ore two beds are known to be present.

Parallel and near to the red fossiliferous, there has been developed along the base of

Mountain Passes of the Cumberland

Cumberland Mountain a superior brown ore, the Limonite—the same as that used in the Low Moor, Longdale, and other furnaces of the Clifton Forge district. This—the Oriskany—has been traced to within ten miles of the company's lands, and there is every reason to believe that it will be developed on them. At the beginning of this article it was stated that iron of superior quality was formerly made at Big Creek Gap, and found a ready market throughout central Kentucky.

Parallel with the ore and easily quarriable is the subcarboniferous limestone, one thick stratum of which contains 98 per cent. of carbonate of lime; so that, with liberal allowance for the cost of crude material, interest, wear and tear, it is estimated that iron can here be made at as low a cost as anywhere in the United States, and that furnaces will have an advantage in freight in reaching the markets of the Ohio Valley and the farther South. Moreover, the various timbers of this region attain a perfection seldom equalled, and by a little clearing out of the stream, logs can be floated at flood tides to the Clinch and Tennessee rivers. To-day mills are shipping these timbers from Boston to the Rocky Mountains.

Situated in one of the most beautiful of valleys, 1200 feet above sea-level, surrounded

Mountain Passes of the Cumberland

by park-like forests and fertile valley lands, having an abundance of pure water and perfect drainage, with iron ore only a mile from coke, and a double water-gap giving easy passage for railroads, Big Creek Gap develops peculiar strength and possibilities of importance, when its relation is shown to those cities which will be its natural markets, and to the systems of railroads of which it will be the inevitable outlet. Within twenty miles of it lie three of the greatest railroad systems of the South. It is but thirty-eight miles from Knoxville, and eight miles of low-grade road, through a fertile blue-grass valley, peopled by intelligent, prosperous farmers, will put it in connection with magnetic and specular ores for the making of steel, or with the mountain of Bessemer ore at Cranberry. Its coke is about three hundred miles nearer to the Sheffield and Decatur furnaces than the Pocahontas coke, which is now being shipped to them. It is nearer St. Louis and Chicago than their present sources of supply. It is the nearest point to the great coaling-station for steamships now building at Brunswick. And it is one of the nearest bases of supply for Pensacola, which in turn is the nearest port of supply for Central and South America.

No element of wealth or advantage of posi-

Mountain Passes of the Cumberland

tion seems lacking to make this place one of the controlling points of that vast commercial movement which is binding the North and the South together, and changing the relation of Kentucky to both, by making it the great highway of railway connection, the fresh centre of manufacture and distribution, and the lasting fountain-head of mineral supply.

VI

ATTENTION is thus briefly directed to that line of towns which are springing up, or will in time spring up, in the mountain passes of the Cumberland, and are making the backwoods of Kentucky the fore-front of a new civilization. Through these three passes in the outer wall of Cumberland Mountain, and through that pass at Pineville in the inner wall behind Cumberland Gap—through these four it is believed that there must stream the railroads carrying to the South its timbers and coals; to the North its timbers, coal, and iron; and carrying to both from these towns, as independent centres of manufacture, all those products the crude materials of which exist in economic combinations on the spot.

It is idle to say that all these places cannot become important. The competition will be keen, and the fittest will survive; but all these are fit to survive, each having advantages of its own. Big Stone Gap lies so much nearer

Mountain Passes of the Cumberland

the East and the Atlantic seaboard; Big Creek Gap so much nearer the West and the Ohio and Mississippi valleys and the Lakes; Cumberland Gap and Pineville so much nearer an intermediate region.

But as the writer has stated, it is the human, not the industrial, problem to be solved by this development that possessed for him the main interest. One seems to see in the perforation and breaking up of Cumberland Mountain an event as decisive of the destiny of Kentucky as though the vast wall had fallen, destroying the isolation of the State, bringing into it the new, and letting the old be scattered until it is lost. But while there is no space here to deal with those changes that are rapidly passing over Kentucky life and obliterating old manners and customs, old types of character and ideals of life, old virtues and graces as well as old vices and horrors—there is a special topic too closely connected with the foregoing facts not to be considered: the effect of this development upon the Kentucky mountaineers.

The buying up of the mountain lands has unsettled a large part of these people. Already there has been formed among them a class of tenants paying rent and living in their old homes. But in the main there are three

Mountain Passes of the Cumberland

movements among them. Some desert the mountains altogether, and descend to the Bluegrass Region with a passion for farming. On county-court days in blue-grass towns it has been possible of late to notice this peculiar type mingling in the market-places with the traditional type of blue-grass farmer. There is thus going on, especially along the border counties, a quiet interfusion of the two human elements of the Kentucky highlander and the Kentucky lowlander, so long distinct in blood, physique, history, and ideas of life. To less extent, the mountaineers go farther west, beginning life again beyond the Mississippi.

A second general tendency among them is to be absorbed by the civilization that is springing up in the mountains. They flock to these towns, keep store, are shrewd and active speculators in real estate, and successful developers of small capital. The first business house put up in the new Pineville was built by a mountaineer.

But the third, and, as far as can be learned, the most general movement among them is to retire at the approach of civilization to remoter regions of the mountains, where they may live without criticism or observation their hereditary, squalid, unambitious, stationary life. But to these retreats they must in time be

Mountain Passes of the Cumberland

followed, therefrom dislodged, and again set going. Thus a whole race of people are being scattered, absorbed, civilized. You may go far before you will find a fact so full of consequences to the future of the State.

Within a few years the commonwealth of Kentucky will be a hundred years old. All in all, it would seem that with the close of its first century the old Kentucky passes away; and that the second century will bring in a new Kentucky — new in many ways, but new most of all on account of the civilization of the Cumberland.

THE END